THE LAVENDER BLADE

Delights and Desires

by Angus Whyte

edited by thomas grexa phillips

Published by Whyte Light Press
First Edition

Books by Angus Whyte

After - Dinner Tales

The Lavender Blade

THE LAVENDER BLADE

Delights and Desires

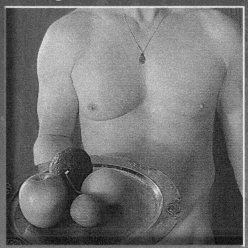

Angus Whyte

The Lavender Blade

Angus Whyte

Edited by thomas grexa phillips, thomgrexaphillips@mac.com

Cover photo by Jeff Reid

Interior and Cover design by Mark E. Anderson

AquaZebra™
Web, Book & Print Design

AquaZebra.com

Published by Whyte Light Press

ISBN: 978-1-954604-01-8

Library of Congress Control Number: 2021904250

First Edition
First Printing, March 2021

Printed in the United States of America

Foreword
By thomas grexa phillips

Thank you, Dear Reader, for your curiosity regarding Angus' tales, and for your support of his memory. Angus Whyte (1937–2019) was larger-than-life in his appetite for delight, for excitement, and in his desires. After embracing some twenty years with him as his spouse, confidant, supporter, and lover, I experienced in him myriad expressions of energy. I often remarked that he came out of the birth canal with his hands on his hips; with an assurance sometimes bordering on swagger, he *never* appreciated being told *what* to do.

Angus dedicated himself to bettering his circumstances and sharing all he had with those around him. His generosity to others was boundless; to himself, not as much. His hearty, humorous, and charismatic demeanor often belied a deep longing for what he *didn't* have. In an unpublished memoir, *Mind Walk,* he lamented his judgmental and punishing mind. Through many sessions of psychotherapy, Angus divined his spirit animal, the Crow, and in the memoir, he reported that the Crow asked him,

Why are you on this endless treadmill of dismay?
Why are you so impatient?

Notwithstanding the Crow Dialogues, his boundless, impatient creativity in our years together did spur him on to further accomplishments, including his stewardship of a community benefit organization that accepted original works of art by donation. The charity, under his leadership, assisted in the installation of art pieces in hospitals and healing centers, which employed them in the creation of healing spaces. Many health-related institutions in the San Francisco Bay Area are the fortunate recipients of his charitable efforts.

Later, Angus accepted a fellowship at an art retreat in France, his spirit country, which inspired him to write and to publish his first collection of stories, *After-Dinner Tales,* in 2013. After moving to Palm Springs in 2017, he became active with music and arts, joined the Palm Springs Writers Guild, and began crafting and polishing the stories enclosed.

The edited collection you are reading is an assemblage of anecdotes, vignettes, and reminiscences that span some sixty years of his lively and interesting life. It was his intention that this publication be dedicated to the "lavender" aspect of his lusty and courageous life.

"Too much is just enough," he would often announce to his many acolytes-in-desire. It is my wish that these *Tales of Delight and Desire* entertain and enlighten you in a similar fashion.

— January, 2021. Cathedral City, CA

Table of Contents

Mary Dee
1957

In 1954 I matriculated at U.C. Berkeley. I was seventeen years old and thrilled to be there, even though I had to work my way through. It was a challenge at times, and the jobs I worked and people I met were as educational as my studies.

During the first semester, I joined a fraternity, but not the one I wished to join, where my four best friends from high school were members. I wasn't invited to their fraternity, and that came as a huge surprise and nasty shock. I didn't know for more than twenty years why I had not been invited, until one of them told me about the huge fight that occurred within their ranks. It turned out I was refused entry because my mother was Jewish—a reason I had never thought to contemplate, it was so outrageous. Our high school was completely integrated, as were our grammar and junior high schools. Black, White, Asian, Latino, rich, poor, smart, and not-so-smart were all part of the fabric of the California school system; I had never experienced prejudice. For several months I was broken-hearted, and then I joined another fraternity simply because they invited me, not because I wanted to be there. Returning late one night, the house was dark except for a light in the kitchen. I went in to turn off the light, and to my surprise and delight, I saw a beautiful young man, completely naked, mopping the floor.

I excused myself for barging in; however, he was totally at ease and said he didn't mind. I asked him why he was mopping the floor naked, and he responded that it felt good to be naked, and he hadn't expected anyone else to be there. We chatted for a while as he continued his mopping. He told me his name was Bill, and during the next couple of weeks and months, we became friends. It turned out that he didn't like the fraternity any more than I did, so we both decided to leave gracefully at the end of the term and find an apartment near the campus.

1

We did, in fact, locate a large, wonderful old apartment on Channing Street, where we remained for the rest of our undergraduate studies. Bill was studying architecture; I was studying French, music, art, and Abnormal Psychology, as any self-respecting gay boy would do in an attempt to find out why we were different.

Bill was not gay, and it didn't make any difference in our friendship. We had our own rooms, mutual friends from Berkeley, Stanford, and the California College of Arts and Crafts in Oakland. He had his girlfriends; I had a few girlfriends and quite a few boyfriends. It was all open, above-board, and tremendous fun.

Bill introduced me to the beauties of architecture and invited me to lectures by Frank Lloyd Wright and Philip Johnson, and I introduced him to classical and baroque music, poetry, fine art, and readings by Marianne Moore.

Our friend Violet Chew, a tall, elegant woman, was studying with Richard Diebenkorn at Arts and Crafts, and I bought my first oil painting from Violet for a hundred dollars—ten installments of ten dollars each. Then I bought a second, in the same way. About forty years later, it occurred to me I was stupid for not having bought a Diebenkorn painting, but it seemed beyond my reach at the time.

Meanwhile, I worked at odd jobs while continuing my classes. The University Placement Office maintained a job board, and notices were posted daily for those who needed or wanted to work. During my senior year I did painting jobs, yard work, wall washing, cleaning, musical gigs, and best—or worst—of all, market promotions for Spreckels Sugar Company. The father of one of my former fraternity brothers, a salesman for Spreckels, took a liking to me and thought I was responsible, which, in truth, I was.

He engaged me to pick up a vehicle on weekends, take a machine supplied by The Company, and spend full days at supermarket openings throughout the Bay Area. I prepared cotton candy for distribution to endless queues of children whose parents were spending money at the supermarkets. The children were usually greedy and unruly—not much fun to deal with—and I was usually stuck in a drafty corridor, large enough to accommodate the crowds enjoying the freebies. By the end of the day, I would be covered with sugar debris and worn out from the work and pressure. But it was worth it because he paid me $125 per day—a fortune at the time. When the work was finished, I had to drive the car an hour or two or three back to Berkeley. To this day, I can't bear the look or smell of spun sugar, grateful as I was at the time for the job.

To supplement that work, I did odd jobs posted on the board. Sometimes I played the piano at Larry Blake's on Telegraph Avenue; they didn't actually pay, but I was fed far too much beer and pizza, and survived on tips. One sweet lady, Mrs. Rogers, hired me to mow her lawn, weed, and maintain her yard once a week. That was a delight compared to the other jobs because it was outdoors and satisfying, but of course it didn't pay as well.

One day, while I was working at Mrs. Rogers' house, a large, shiny, brand-new, black Buick sedan pulled up in front of the house, and an elegantly-attired, beautiful woman, probably about thirty, disembarked and went inside. Shortly after, Mrs. Rogers introduced me to the woman, who was her sister-in-law. She was called Mary Dee, and before she left, she asked for my telephone number in case she could provide any additional work. Happy to oblige, I gave her my number. The next day she telephoned and asked me to visit her at home, which turned out to be a large, handsome house in the Berkeley hills.

Alone in the house, she offered me a cup of coffee, asked me what I was studying, then showed me the yard and the garden shed where the mower and tools were kept, and she suggested I begin work there. It seemed to me that the yard was already in fine shape and did not require much in the way of mowing. She informed me that the gardener took care of the yard, and perhaps I could teach her how to pronounce the names of all the French wines in her husband's cellar. We abandoned the yard and moved into the cellar, which was extensive and excellent. I did my best to teach her a rudimentary French pronunciation, and she suggested we take a bottle upstairs to try it out.

This was all quite fascinating, and I told her I'd feel better if I at least cleaned up the dead leaves in the garden. I went back to the garden and began clearing away the leaves, when I suddenly noticed her standing on a balcony above, watching me. I waved, and she said: "It's awfully warm, wouldn't you feel better taking off your shirt?"

By this time I was beginning to get what was happening, so I took off my shirt and replied, "Maybe it's time to try out that wine now." I climbed the stairs to the balcony. It was about 10:30 in the morning by then, and we tucked into the wine, a deliciously-aged Burgundy.

We talked more. She told me her husband was a dentist, they had three boys who were in private school, she had almost died during the birth of the third boy, and her doctor told her it was not advisable for her to have any more children and gave her a hysterectomy. Consequently, her husband lost interest in her sexually and emotionally, and she was, except for the sake of propriety, alone. Her husband gave her the Buick, as much money as she needed or wanted for clothing, jewelry, and fine dining, and left her to her own resources.

She was a lovely woman, slender, with honey-colored hair, usually pulled up into a French twist, and of course I felt sorry for her; and of course she was deprived and needy. We then, gradually, embarked on an "affairette." She remained at home in the evenings with the children, and during the day, she was totally free. Two or three times a week, she would meet me at Sather Gate at midday with the Buick, and we would go off to a quiet, elegant little restaurant far from her neighborhood. She would slip me a twenty-dollar bill, so I could be The Man paying for lunch, and then we'd go back to my apartment and have sex. Lots of sex.

In those days, no one ever locked their doors, and sometimes in the afternoon, when I returned after classes, I would find steaks, fresh vegetables, peaches, watermelons, strawberries, lovely wines, and various treats which she had left during the day. Bill and I, along with many of our friends, were the grateful beneficiaries of Mary's largesse that year.

The future was not a topic for discussion. It was clear that I would graduate and go away, and Mary would, of course, remain in Berkeley. We took advantage of the moments we had and enjoyed them thoroughly.

Shortly before my graduation, Mary offered to host a party in our apartment. My mother and sister came to the event, as did my aunt, uncle, cousin, boyfriends, girlfriends, Bill of course, and the girl who had invited me to the Prom. The bathtub was filled with bottles of French champagne, and platters from the best local delicatessen were offered, along with and fabulous pastries.

When it became time to leave for the Prom, I knew this was the bittersweet end of my relationship with Mary. So did she, and it was sad, as well as inevitable.

The following day I left for a summer job, working in a Rockefeller resort in Jackson Hole, Wyoming, Then I began a hitch-hiking trip across the country to Boston, New York, Miami, New Orleans . . . and the beginning of my adult life.

Hotel Uniek

1963

In the autumn of 1963 I arrived in Amsterdam for a year of study at the Conservatory of Music. It was my first time there, and one of my gay friends in Boston suggested I stay at the Hotel Uniek. I had reserved a room there for my first week to have a base while looking for a more permanent domicile in the city.

My Boston friend had also given me the names of two gay clubs to visit—the COC and the DOK. After unpacking, showering, and changing clothes, I went off to explore Amsterdam and locate the clubs. When I arrived at the DOK, I was astonished to find an upscale, contemporary, beautifully-designed and appointed space. It had a mirrored wall on one side reflecting the bar, a small dance floor, a restaurant with white napkins and tablecloths, and waiters wearing black trousers, white shirts, and bow ties—a far cry from the dirty, dingy, hole-in-the-walls in San Francisco, New York, and Boston, always hidden away in the crummiest parts of town.

It didn't take me long to learn it was perfectly all right to be openly gay in the Netherlands, with clubs that were friendly, clean, and happily international; with men from England, Germany, France, Switzerland, Italy and elsewhere enjoying the freedoms and atmospheres not found at home. Genever, the world's original gin, remains popular since Heer Bols, Rembrandt's friend and neighbor, invented it in the seventeenth century. It was easy for me to develop a taste for Genever as well as Rembrandt's paintings in the Rijksmuseum.

By the end of my first evening at the DOK, I found a handsome Dutch boy who was willing to come back to the hotel with me. He stayed the night, and early in the morning we heard a knock, the door opened, and a terribly cute waiter brought in a tray with two breakfasts for us. My first day there, and I was already hooked on Dutch hospitality. I'm still fond of Dutch breakfasts: fresh coffee, a hard roll, a soft-boiled egg, and Gouda cheese with maybe a slice or two of ham.

During the first few days, I looked for an apartment, visited the museums, and walked endlessly, enchanted by the canals, architecture, ancient houses and buildings, and herring stands on the corners. For the first three nights, I went to the club and returned to the hotel with a new friend, and each morning the waiter brought in breakfast for two. By the fourth night, I was exhausted and returned to the hotel early for a good night's sleep. Early in the morning, the knock came, and the waiter arrived with two breakfasts. Surprised, he laughed; I told him I was unable to eat two breakfasts alone and he had better get in bed and have breakfast with me.

He set down the tray, took off his clothes, and we had a bit more than breakfast in the bed. I understood just how "unique" the hotel was, in fact. Its name was well deserved!

Vows of Silence

for Robert A. Johnson
1964

While completing my M.A. Degree at the University of
Washington, I signed up for piano lessons from Else Geissmar,
a German lady who had fled her homeland at the beginning
of WWII and then settled in Seattle. A strict technician and
precise taskmaster—as one might have expected from a Teutonic
musical dominatrix—with iron fingers on her tiny hands, she
spoke in a heavily-accented English. Fortunately, she possessed
a quirky sense of humor as well as splendid musicianship, and
I enjoyed her company as well as my lessons and rapid progress
with her.

Else was not the only European musician who had sought
refuge at the university, and I soon enjoyed the experience of
meeting and getting to know her colleague, Eva Heinitz, an
expert cellist and master of the viola da gamba. Eva's English was
less accomplished, but her memories of her journey to America
were fantastic, and those tales, both musical and historical, were
legendary. A stout woman—almost square in shape—when she
sat down to play, Eva became simply angelic.

Within a few years of her arrival, Eva had transformed the
music department at the university, and during the summer, she
performed at the Bach Festival in Carmel, California. In addition to her German background and remarkable technique,
she brought a great love for Bach, and for Baroque Music. She
somehow managed, in the early 1950s, to put together a group of
musicians to join her in presenting programs featuring recorders,
harpsichords, lutenists, a consort of viols, and other baroque
instruments—instruments and sounds previously unknown
to many of us at that time. Entranced by the sounds of these
unfamiliar keyboards, with dark keys where the white ones typically are on a piano, and white ones where the black keys usually

reside, I ordered a virginal, my first plucked-string instrument, by mail from the English builder, Alec Hodsdon, in 1959.

Meanwhile, I completed my Master of Arts degree, received a Fulbright Scholarship to study in France, and during that year, made a trip to Lavenham, Suffolk, to visit Mr. Hodsdon while he was building the instrument. Thus began my rocky career as a harpsichordist.

Returning from France in the summer of 1960, I pursued a doctoral program in French Literature and Civilization at UCLA, where I also planned to study the harpsichord. My experience in the academic environment turned out to be less than pleasant and led me to abandon an academic life. In a lucky quirk of fate, just as I was about to flee UCLA, the U.S. Government sent a letter to French departments in a number of major universities requesting single, male persons who were fluent in French. They were needed to participate in government-sponsored gift programs to nine, newly-independent African nations. Each of the nine nations had the option to receive a Mobile Medical Vehicle or a Mobile Cinema Vehicle. Both were designed to travel out of cities and into remote areas, many without electricity. Several of the larger nations were to receive both vehicles.

My great friend and ally Marina Preussner, the Russian secretary of the UCLA French Department, in her infinite wisdom persuaded me to complete the term, apply for the government program, and thereby receive a letter of recommendation from the chairman of the department, all while making a graceful exit from UCLA. Accepted into the program, I attended a summer crash course in African Studies at Indiana University as preparation. After that, I went on assignment for a year to the Congo Republic, where I was given a modified Jeep filled with mobile cinema equipment. I was instructed to choose a team of young Congolese and teach them, in French, to operate the equipment; to repair film damaged in the harsh, equatorial climate; and to program tours into remote Congo bush country to show "educational" films in regions without electricity to people who had never seen a film. It was clear from my second week in Brazzaville that the minister of education coveted the vehicle, and that the minute my job was complete and I was out of the picture, the vehicle would be his. Whatever programs had begun during my tenure would end with my departure.

Returning to the U.S. in the late spring of 1961, I found a job in Salinas replacing—for the remainder of the semester— a French teacher at the local high school who left suddenly on maternity leave. Thanks to a suggestion by undergraduate friends from Berkeley, Donna and Richard Sloan, who were then living just south of Monterey, I found a room, rented a harpsichord, and decided to seriously practice the instrument and learn the literature. With another stroke of good luck, I met and became friendly with Alan Curtis, a baroque scholar and fine harpsichordist on the faculty at UC Berkeley, who agreed to give me weekly lessons. Alan introduced me to the keyboard music of Louis Couperin, François Couperin, Domenico Scarlatti, Antonio Soler, Sweelinck, Bach (of course), and a host of lesser lights in the baroque stellar firmament. He encouraged my musical sophistication by playing entire Handel and Monteverdi operas as we watched the scores, as well as generally laying out the history and development of several hundred years of glorious keyboard music not only by listening, but by performing it.

During the summer, Donna and Richard introduced me to a gentleman farmer named Wolterding, proprietor of Rancho Rico in Big Sur, who invited me there to spend the summer. He claimed a great love of music and wanted to "help me with my career." He was a closet case of vast proportions and a recovering Christian Scientist. He professed adherence to the tenets of that organization, but he liked to drink secretly. He would throw empty wine bottles into a ravine on his ranch and sneak into my room in the middle of the night, uninvited, to "help my career" with a clandestine blowjob in my "sleep." His hypocrisy bothered me far more than the blowjobs, and I became uncomfortable with the situation.

After a week or so at the ranch, Wolterding invited two of

his neighbors for dinner, Emile Norman and Brooks Clement. Emile was an artist, and Brooks an accomplished photographer, carpenter, electrician, and businessman. They had been partners for fifteen years and had built their own house and studio on nearby Pfeiffer Ridge. Handsome, sexy, funny and smart, they were incredibly compelling, and the next day, wearing only a pair of shorts, I set off to find their house. It was a long way— much farther than I'd anticipated—and I arrived parched, sunburned, and hungry. They gave me something to eat and drink, and before I knew it, we were all in the pool—naked. I stayed with them for a glorious year.

When I brought my things over, Emile was entranced by the Hodsdon virginal and asked if he could make a wood inlay in the lid. I was thrilled, and during the next month or two, he imagined the grain in the walnut lid as a sunset and inlaid. With tiny pieces of rare woods and ivory, he accomplished his plan: a setting sun and a flock of birds flying below, as if to emulate the sounds emanating out of the instrument. By this time, my harpsichord proficiency was improving, and the small, rented harpsichord was becoming unsatisfactory. Alan Curtis had introduced me to the beauties of modern, handmade harpsichords by Frank Hubbard, Bill Dowd, and Martin Skowronick. I also developed a deep yearning for an authentic, eighteenth century instrument and began to make inquiries as to where I might find one.

My research led to Robert Johnson, a Jungian analyst in Los Angeles, who loved baroque music and instruments. He represented the Neupert organization in the US. (Wittmayer and Neupert were two German companies then making commercial harpsichords and spinets.) A very gentle man, Bob was shy, calm, quiet, and deliberate. He moved slowly, due to an injury which had cost him one leg, and he was delighted in my interest in finding an ancient instrument. He owned a double-manual Ruckers, an early eighteenth-century Flemish instrument, which was entrancing, both visually and acoustically. Almost miraculously, within a month or so, he had located a single-manual

Kirckman harpsichord from 1764, which was available for $2,500. Emile lent me part of the money to buy it, and we had it delivered to the studio in Big Sur.

Bowed and warped by two hundred years of pressure from the strings stretched over the soundboard, it was a gorgeous sight to behold. The walnut case was dark with age, and the brass fittings had not been polished for decades. Emile was appalled when I told him the first project I intended to do was polish the brass. He was worried about ruining the patina. I told him that the brass fittings and hinges were meant to contrast with the wood, not resemble it, and I set about polishing them all. Because of the age of the instrument, I could never bring them back to what they had looked like originally, but they cleaned up successfully and gleamed splendidly against the dark walnut.

Next, we began to examine the strings and action. Like a virginal, the unique sound of a harpsichord is produced by a tiny plectrum made of quill lodged in a mechanism on the jack, the wooden shaft which rises and falls as the string is plucked on the way up after the key is struck. A tiny spring on the back of the jack allows the quill mechanism to slide over the string on the return without making a sound, and a small piece of felt damps the sound of the string as the jack returns to its base position. The quills on the Kirckman were in terrible condition, and due to warping of the frame, a significant number of notes were unplayable.

My responsibility, as part of the household, was to help Emile make woodblock prints whenever he was in the mood for that. At other times, when he was sculpting or painting, I was free to practice and work on the Kirckman. During the summer, I restrung the entire instrument, which had three sets of strings. I renovated the action, put new springs on the jacks, replaced the felt dampers, and filed the jacks where they rubbed or jammed against the rails.

Robert sent me a treatise entitled "The Gentle Art of Quilling," which began with a sentence stating that quills were best prepared from feathers obtained from "a middle-aged crow or raven." The second sentence was, "Prepare the quills as you would for a pen." Because I had no access to middle-aged crows or ravens, nor any idea how to make a pen, I collected seagull feathers from the beach. I trimmed the feathers and learned how to make a pen. With that exercise satisfactorily accomplished, I practiced making quills and eventually quilled the entire instrument with seagull plectra. (Alan told me that his teacher and mentor, Gustav Leonhardt, quilled his seventeenth and eighteenth century instruments with condor quills obtained from the Amsterdam zoo.)

The first concert on the renovated Kirckman—with a soprano, oboist, and cellist from the Carmel Bach Festival—was a great success. The house and studio were all made of wood, the acoustics were not unlike those of an English or French salon, and the instrument looked and sounded golden.

In the course of time, I learned why seagull feather quills are not often used: they wear out quickly. Alan introduced me to Delrin, a plastic material which, when shaved and trimmed, resembles quill and lasts much longer. (Harpsichord builders, I was told, don't like the word "Delrin" and tend to call it either "Goosite" or "Crowflex.") As the seagull plectra wore out, I gradually replaced them all with Delrin. The sound remained the same, but the plectra, happily, didn't wear out for years.

My interest and delight in baroque keyboard music continued. I performed several times at Berkeley, as well as privately in San Francisco and around the Bay Area. Alan encouraged me to apply for a grant to study at the Amsterdam Conservatory with Gustav Leonhardt. I received an Alfred Hertz grant and left Big Sur, reluctantly and with great excitement, in the fall of 1963.

The year in Amsterdam—followed by an extension of the grant to attend summer courses at the Mozarteum Academy in Salzburg—was glorious. In addition to my harpsichord studies, I was given the opportunity to practice and play some of the finest baroque organs in the world, not only in Amsterdam but in Haarlem, Alkmaar, and elsewhere. To his students, Leonhardt was a magisterial figure, personally and musically, and we all believed him to be the reincarnation of the great seventeenth-century Dutch composer and performer, Jan Pieterszoon Sweelinck. In addition to teaching and serving as mentor and example, Leonhardt also gained access for us to visit the collections of ancient instruments in The Hague, Paris, Munich, Salzburg, and Vienna. We were able to perform on period instruments, including some of Mozart's and Beethoven's pianos, as well as the surviving and renovated great instruments from England, Germany, the Netherlands, Austria, France, Italy and Spain. These instruments included harpsichords, virginals, spinets, clavichords, chamber organs, and unusual instruments such as the clavicytherium (an upright harpsichord) and the giraffe (an upright grand piano). It was a heady year, in every way!

While studying in Amsterdam, I was encouraged by Leonhardt to order a modern harpsichord, in addition to the Kirckman. Skowroneck's waiting list was ten years, Hubbard's and Dowd's were each five years, so I ordered a new, two-manual, Flemish-style harpsichord from Rainer Schütze, a builder in Heidelberg who promised to have the instrument completed in a year. Following a series of miscommunications for a period—due to his poor English and my poor German—I finally went to Heidelberg to visit him when the instrument had been partially finished. As promised, the completed harpsichord was delivered to me in San Francisco in the fall of 1964. Thus began the demise of my career as a harpsichordist, but I didn't realize that for another seven years.

Having grown accustomed to small halls in castles and grand houses in Amsterdam, Salzburg, Vienna, Paris, and London, I was disappointed to discover San Francisco had little to offer in the way of appropriate settings for baroque music. I played on houseboats in Sausalito, in coffee shops in San Francisco, on the radio, on television, and with friends. To make a living, however, I had to teach, like so many musicians, and moonlight doing catering work. Though lucrative, this took a toll on my self-image.

Interestingly, as a harpsichordist, one loses patience with

loud sounds. Most modern pianos sound vulgar in comparison, and the habit of applause, which most audiences demand, diminishes the enjoyment of a clavichord or harpsichord program. I frequently asked audiences to *not* applaud until the end of a program, but people found it impossible to resist when they were pleased.

A high point of that period was a visit to Robert Johnson in Three Rivers, Michigan, where he had become a Lay Brother at a Benedictine Monastery. He was, like all monks, obliged to take vows of poverty, and did so with two exceptions: he refused to give up his beloved 1714 Ruckers harpsichord, a Flemish instrument of extraordinary beauty, and his newly acquired modern German clavichord.

Whereas my Kirckman had a typically English, golden, rich, round, resonant sound, Bob's Ruckers had a silvery, almost etched, crystalline sound, unmatched in my experience. Although a connoisseur of baroque music, because of his shy and retiring nature, Bob did not enjoy performing in public. He invited me to visit him at the monastery and to perform for the brothers on his Ruckers. I was thrilled to accept his invitation.

Upon arrival, I was startled when Bob welcomed me in a brown monastic robe. It hadn't occurred to me that he'd be dressed like a monk. He motioned for me to follow him, took me aside, and explained that all the monks in that monastery had taken vows of silence. That had also not occurred to me, my experience with monasteries at the time being non-existent. I asked if they were permitted to speak at meals, and he said no. A reader, he explained, read aloud during communal meals, but conversation was not possible. I asked, "What do you do if you want the salt?"

He replied, "Someone will pass it to you. Simply be aware of your neighbors." A novel concept for me then. I found the meals surprisingly enjoyable.

When it came time for my performance, Bob warned me not to be disappointed, for there would be no applause. Of course I was overjoyed. For the first and only time in my life, the audience of robed monks filed in silently, sat silently, and waited silently for the music to begin. I began with a suite by Louis Couperin. The unmeasured prelude at the beginning of the suite, followed by the delicately precise dances, sounded almost as they might have when they were first written. The program progressed with several Scarlatti sonatas and concluded with Bach's French Suite No. 4. Without interruptions from applause or conversation, the sounds from the Ruckers seemed to grow and expand exponentially, filling every nook and cranny of the small chapel. As a performer, I had never experienced anything like it. It seemed balanced and perfect, thanks to the vows of silence.

The only time during my visit that Bob and I could carry on a conversation was to whisper in his cell. Following the concert, he invited me there to see and hear his German clavichord. In addition to the fact that it was a beautiful instrument, Bob had carved a rose in the soundboard and wanted to show it off.

A harpsichord, in comparison to a clavichord, is loud. The instrument is shaped somewhat like a grand piano, except the edges of the case are usually angled rather than curved. Harpsichord strings are plucked by plectra, and two or sometimes three sets of strings on a large, double-manual instrument may be engaged simultaneously, creating a rich and sonorous resonance. In contrast, a clavichord is much smaller and rectangular in shape. It has only one set of strings which are struck by small brass tangents, and the sound produced is almost inaudible—which is why clavichord concerts are so rare: a clavichord is almost impossible to hear from more than a foot away. Another difference is that, because clavichords have no dampers, a performer has the option of holding the tangents against the strings, and by moving their fingers up and down vertically, they may create a vibrato effect. When properly played, the sound is fragile, cantabile, and lovely, although almost too quiet for modern ears.

As Bob played pieces he loved, demonstrating the qualities of the instrument and its sounds, I noticed a box-like shape resting on the open lid—something I'd never seen on any such instrument. When he'd finished playing, I whispered, "Bob, what is that box on top of the instrument?"

His face reddened slightly. He paused, and whispered back, "It's a mute."

In disbelief, I replied stupidly, "A *mute?* On a *clavichord?*"

This time he blushed and whispered back, "You've got to understand, because of the vows of silence here, the sound this thing makes is *deafening!*"

Rated X

1969

Eddie and I were finishing supper last night at our neighborhood Chinese restaurant.

We've been living together now for almost five years, and it's a bit of a bore to cook at home every night, even though both of us cook well and can easily whip up anything, from a simple grilled hamburger to an exquisite French sauce. We both think it's important to have at least one civilized meal a day. Because of our jobs and the usual everyday rush, it's almost impossible to be civilized at any meal but dinner. In fact, we invite friends to dinner almost three nights out of five—occasionally it's planned, but more often it's just a casual thing. We've learned it's the best way to get together with our gay friends outside the bars. Oh sure, we go to the bars too, but that whole scene is so artificial we feel it's necessary to make a costume project of it— tight pants and sweaters to the college-boy bars; bells and beads to the freak bar; Levis, boots and leather to the motorcycle bars; and then, once in a while, we wear the wrong thing to a bar, hoping it will amuse everyone, turn them on, blow their minds, offend them, or all of the above.

When we entertain at home, it's usually casual, comfortable, and relaxed. No artificial tensions are created by the bar atmosphere, so an unstructured evening can develop and progress naturally. We have a drink or two, but it's rare for anyone to get drunk anymore. We smoke sometimes, talk a lot, and listen to records—all sorts, including pop, rock, baroque, and other foreign and exotic sounds. Sometimes we play word games and write verses or communal poems, and often we organize chamber music ensembles or read plays or stories we've written. We include lots of camp, far too much double entendre, and, of course, complete histories of what the world has done or is doing in, on, and around The Bed.

Eddie and I are now generally considered a "couple," and that's fine with both of us. When we first dated, seven years ago, it was just for sex. We seldom went out or socialized then; we just went to bed. (Now, I maintain that our relationship is solidly based on the firmest possible mutual interest: sex.) It's turned out, fortunately, that we like each other too. When I returned from a year of study in Europe, Eddie's roommate decided to move away. That's when Eddie and I, almost accidentally, decided to share an apartment. We looked and looked, but we couldn't find an apartment we liked or could afford that had two bedrooms. (Originally, we thought we'd have less static from prospective landlords if we asked for two bedrooms.) Fate intervened, however, and we found just the right apartment with one bedroom. We moved in with one bed, and now, five years and several apartments later, we still sleep in one bed, except if one of us wants to trick, or a mother or mother-in-law comes to visit.

We have discussed almost everything about being gay and living together. We've decided the only way we can make it work is to be perfectly honest about everything. If one of us is unhappy, we talk about it. If both of us are happy, we talk about that as well, but not too much. If one of us meets someone sexy and wants to trick, we don't pretend it isn't happening. It happens . . . usually separately, but sometimes together. (Fortunately, we seldom agree on the ultimate sex appeal of a single individual, nor have we ever had to resort to the ten-point scale to rate our preferences.) Little rivalry exists between us, and if there is just a bit, it's even more exciting because, eventually, we'll both win out.

During our five years together, almost everything has happened at least once: family tragedies, arguments, separate vacations, job problems, automobile accidents, small jealousies, trips to Europe, trips to Mexico, sex in the car, sex in the park, sex in bed, sex on the floor. We've had twosomes, threesomes, foursomes, orgies, grass, mescaline, and poppers. We've fucked and been fucked, sucked and been sucked, rimmed, sixty-nined, saunaed and steam-bathed. We've done it in the shower; we've done it in the woods; we've done it at the beach. (We haven't yet done it in the road, but that will happen.) We've done it with students, truck drivers, cops, cowboys, hairdressers, ribbon clerks, soldiers, sailors, window dressers, musicians, actors, dancers, composers, writers, doctors, psychiatrists, businessmen, bankers, travel agents, boyish men, and even girls. And after all that, separately or together, we still like it. We like to go to bed together. We still turn each other on. We like to wake up together in the morning. We have a good life, and we intend to continue having a good life. We work hard, and we make enough money; we do pretty much what we want. It may not be exactly what Mr. and Mrs. America call a "normal home life," but it's normal for us.

So, last night, as we were finishing supper, on the spur of the moment, we decided to catch the last show at the University Cinema, a rerun of Busby Berkeley's *Gold Diggers of 1933*. Neither of us had previously seen a Busby Berkeley film, although we loved the off-Broadway production of *Dames at Sea*, a delicious spoof of thirties musicals. (In this life, it's almost impossible to be totally unfamiliar with Busby Berkeley, even if you have never seen one of his films.)

The film was a treat, from the too-close close-up of Ginger Rogers' teeth singing, "Eer-way in-lay ee-thay oney-may," through Ruby Keeler's inimitable vocal artistry, to the incredible flower formations of myriad, tiered-skirted chorus girls playing electric violins that glowed in the dark. It was a great film, and, in addition, we learned a lot about the thirties.

Happily humming *The Forgotten Man* theme, we strolled through the lobby toward the exit. Near the door, an obvious university-type theater major stood in front of a publicity poster for the film. He was gesticulating and explaining just a little too loudly to his girlfriend that Busby Berkeley was *not* the producer, he was *only* the choreographer; that Dick Powell had not *really* written all the songs in the film; that "Gold-Diggers" was not, in fact, Berkeley's finest film because . . . and so forth.

Suddenly I became aware of an old man at my side. His hair, gray and unkempt, seemed almost to stand above his head. In need of a shave, looking scruffy at best, he wore a rumpled suit which he had evidently slept in. His one noteworthy feature, which fascinated me instantly was a pair of intense, arresting, blue eyes. "What does he know about it?" he muttered, "He wasn't even born then."

"And you, sir," I inquired. "You must have seen it when it first appeared."

"Indeed I did," he answered.

So I ventured on. "Well, how has it survived? Is it better or worse than when you first saw it?"

"Better!" he responded without hesitation. "A lot better than all the nudity, perversion, and immorality you see in films nowadays."

"Not so," I disagreed.

He frowned and asked, "What do you mean, 'not so'?"

I claimed that the film was simply a visual entertainment and nothing more. He disagreed vehemently, so I felt obliged to ask, "You can't honestly think that film we just saw represents any sort of real-life situations?"

He replied, "Of course it does. It shows that not all chorus girls are wicked."

That was really too much, I thought, especially for someone who had obviously never recovered from the Depression, so I countered with, "That's the most perverted film I ever saw!"

He seemed genuinely taken aback by this observation and said, "Name one scene where there was any perversion."

I answered that the entire film was an esthetically perverted view of reality; furthermore, that nudity in itself was not immoral and that neither nudity in films nor a Busby Berkeley chorus girl was necessarily moral or immoral.

Eddie, who had been waiting patiently through all this, was by this point becoming bored by the encounter and tugged at my elbow. As we began to leave, the old man looked at me angrily and said, "Running off, just like all the boys—running off."

And as we parted, I heard him quietly mutter, as if to himself: "Fellatio, sodomy . . . *that's* perversion." And then, to me, very loudly across the foyer of the theater, "What do you know about perversion anyway?"

My Sochi Night
1970

Tom and Sally, my friends who live in London and love to travel, invited me and my boyfriend, Eddie, to join them and a group they had assembled for a trip to the Soviet Union in 1970—long before it became popular or easy to do. In fact, the rules were strict. Travelers were required to arrive and depart in groups. Our group included two families with young children and Sally's distinguished uncle (who gained fame for playing Batman's butler on television). I also invited my mother to join us for what would be her first trip to Europe and beyond. We planned to stop in London on the way over and visit Paris on the return, so if the Soviet adventure proved to be a bust, at least we would enjoy an excellent beginning and end to the trip.

We all congregated in London at the airport and travelled together, first to Moscow for a few days, St. Petersburg for another few days, Sochi on the Black Sea for three days, and lastly Kiev, in the Ukraine, before returning to Europe.

The flight to Moscow on Aeroflot was uneventful, but not promising. The service and meals were erratic and uninteresting. Our arrival in Moscow was at night, and we were bused to our hotel around ten o'clock. We were met by Svetlana, a beautiful young woman who spoke English surprisingly well. She explained she would be our guide for the entire trip. The families with children and the older folks decided to remain in the hotel, and the rest of us were eager to see Red Square and St. Basil's church at night.

We asked Svetlana for directions to the subway, and she told us it was impossible for us to go there, because it wasn't part of the tour itinerary. We repaired to the hotel bar for a drink and waited until she left. Once we were outside, we figured out where the subway was located and arrived at Red

Square in a half-hour. Our initial fondness for Svetlana evaporated almost instantly and was never regained.

———∞∞∞———

Red Square and St. Basil's Cathedral were spectacular in the bright summer evening, and we all agreed the enormous scale of the square, with the onion domes and spires of the cathedral, provided the most phantasmagorical urban sight imaginable. Delighted with our success, we returned to the hotel for the morrow's tour, which was comprised of a series of government buildings (devoid of design or charm) and Svetlana's endless Communist drone and propaganda, which only served to aggravate our dislike of her.

The food in the hotel was so bad that, by the second night, a group of us got together and went out to a local restaurant, where it was no better. In fact, it seemed that all the meals had been prepared in some monstrous central kitchen and transported to the entire country. Soups were thin and watery, fowl was tough and stringy, meat was almost unobtainable and unpalatable when it was available. I had enjoyed fresh caviar several times in New York and Boston, so I expected to find it almost everywhere. Sadly, there was a blight in the Caspian Sea that summer, and fresh caviar was unavailable. It was a huge disappointment, and we had to make do with large quantities of vodka without caviar.

Before our departure, a friend at Harvard who taught Russian and had lived in Moscow, suggested that Eddie and I take along flight bags filled with American bits of clothing, because those items were extremely popular with Russian youths. I packed my PanAm flight bag with a few brightly-colored shirts, Levi blue jeans, a fringed leather cowboy vest, and a few gaudy t-shirts and flashy ties. Our friend also told us that if we wanted to meet guys in Moscow, there was only one way to do it, which was to go to the park directly across from the Bolshoi Ballet and wait until midnight.

We spent the first evening at the Moscow Circus and the

second at the Bolshoi Ballet. Following the ballet, which ended around eleven o'clock, most of our group returned to the hotel. However, Eddie and I decided to stay out and try our luck in the park. We sat down on a park bench. No one was in sight, and we almost left. At the stroke of midnight, the lights went out, and instantly the park was alive with men cruising. We went our separate ways, and we both scored, not meeting again until early the next morning at the hotel.

I had encountered a fair-haired young man who spoke some English as well as French. He invited me back to his room, exhorting utmost silence as we entered, given that some of other occupants of the building were not to be disturbed. I noticed that people generally were fearful and suspicious in Russia. Someone always seemed to be watching or listening. When we arrived in his room, I was startled to see an enormous poster on one wall portraying Richard Nixon. Checking my desire to explain how distasteful I found the image, I realized it was his way of showing his admiration for the U.S. He offered me a drink, put a Pergolesi recording on his player, and we spent the night together, happily improving international relations and heating up the cold war.

Leningrad, which I insisted on calling "St. Petersburg," was chillier than Moscow in every way. The city is beautiful and far more European than Moscow. It was a thrill to visit the Hermitage Museum, even though the halls were dim, lightings were poor, paintings badly lit, and the antique silver, which had not been polished for more than a century. Almost all the guards were asleep at their posts, and there were few visitors, other than our group. Once again, however, the cuisine in St. Petersburg was beyond disappointing; it was awful.

The high point of the trip for me was our visit to Sochi, a popular resort town on the Black Sea. At the beach we saw literally thousands of Russians, mostly heavy set, in bathing costumes, standing in the water, deployed in rows. No one seemed to be swimming; evidently they preferred just standing in the water. On the walk back to the hotel from the beach, two boys approached us. We had no common language; however, it became clear that they wanted to sell an icon. Eddie left in dismay, and I stayed. We sat on a bench, and they furtively pulled the "icon" out of a bag and showed it off. In the first place, I told them, it was far too dangerous for us as Americans to buy anything or for them to sell it, given that the government requires visitors to list every ruble or dollar brought in and account for every expenditure upon departure. I didn't tell them what a miserable piece of art it was, because they were cute and friendly. In fact, I suggested we meet the following day, and perhaps we could affect a trade. The dark-haired boy was Ivan, and his blond pal Pyotr.

In the morning, Svetlana, Eddie and the group embarked for a lengthy bus trip to set foot in Asia, which I thought was a stupid idea. I refused to go, causing Svetlana great anxiety—to my immense delight. After they left, I packed the flight bag with all my "subversive" American gear and met the boys in the afternoon. We undressed, swam, and lay on the beach. Pyotr was an athlete and swimmer, with a beautiful smooth body and a tiny tattoo on his left shoulder that resembled a hyphen. I queried him about its meaning, and he quietly explained that it referred to the central bar in the letter H. That seemed odd to me, so he explained further that it meant he was a hippie, but it would be too dangerous for him to have a complete H tattooed on his arm; Russia was still an extremely repressed country at the time. I appreciated the irony of this clean-cut, short-haired, handsome, athletic young guy thinking of himself as a hippie. Hippies in San Francisco and New York did not look like that.

After the swim they took me on a long bus ride to a bar which served warm Georgian sparkling wine, which they called "Georgian Champagne." It was not only warm; it was sweet, sticky and tasteless. However the boys remained cute and friendly. After we had drunk far too much, we found a café with totally forgettable food and décor, and afterwards they invited me back to their digs—in this case, a room on the top floor of an ancient building, where they lived with three other boys.

It was about 110 degrees Fahrenheit in the room, and as soon as we arrived, they all stripped down to their underwear. I couldn't have asked for a better welcome! They served more cheap "Georgian Champagne" and unveiled the icon again, which I pretended to appreciate. Then I opened my flight bag and pulled out the array of flashy American clothing, and each one of them tried on all the clothes, one piece at a time. It was a splendid spectacle in any language—and in this case, no language at all. I couldn't have been happier, except for wishing I had photographs of all the boys in underwear trying on all the American frippery. At about two in the morning, the boys had decided which one would keep which shirt, tie, jeans, fringed jacket or whatever, and I announced it was time for me to go.

They laughed uproariously and informed me that it was too late for the bus. I explained it didn't matter—I would take a taxi. They laughed even harder and told me there were no taxis in Sochi and I would have to spend the night there. That made me nervous. I told them I absolutely had to be back at the hotel by eight o'clock in the morning, otherwise the bus for the plane would leave without me. Besides, I knew that Eddie and my mother would be upset if I weren't there for breakfast. The boys promised me they'd get me back in time, and I had no choice but to remain.

They conferred amongst themselves, pointed to one of the cots, and said I could sleep there. I said it wasn't fair for any of them to give up his space. I pointed to Pyotr and announced that I would sleep with him. They found that vastly amusing, and so it was. We all crashed, and after a suitable delay, Pyotr and I managed to have quiet, furtive sex amid that heat and youthful testosterone. It was delicious. The next morning, we were up at dawn and they escorted me on the bus back to the hotel, as promised.

Not surprisingly, Eddie was furious. He told me he could hardly sleep and was imagining my mutilated corpse in some remote Russian ditch where it couldn't be found. I told him it was the best night of the trip so far and reminded him that he had been invited along but chose not to go. He informed me, with some asperity, that my mother had knocked on the door fifteen minutes earlier, and he'd had to lie and tell her we'd be down shortly. And, in fact, we were.

———∞∞∞———

The adventure continued. We flew to the Ukraine, where the food was slightly better, but not much. We heard *Eugene Onegin* at the Kirov Opera House, where the stout chorus women wore costumes looking like the original nineteenth-century gowns which had been let out repeatedly for some 150 years. That's all I recall from the performance. I was too tired from the previous Sochi night, which was infinitely more memorable.

A Letter to James Lord

1970

Dear James,

I'm back to Boston and back to reality (whatever that means), and I've been meaning to write you for what seems like ages, although I suppose it's only a month or so. First, thank you for all the good will you so generously dispensed. Second, I would like to recount the rest of the adventure that last night I saw you; I didn't have the good fortune to see you and relate it to you in person.

We had taken my mother to lunch, as you no doubt recall. You were terribly affable and completely charming, but we hardly had a chance at all to carry on, so I suggested we meet later at some appropriate watering place. I called you at six-thirty, because you were planning dinner with someone, and you explained how to reach Les Nuages, where we agreed to meet around eleven-thirty.

The place was easy to find and was just where you said it would be. As you'd suggested, I could tell which doorway to go in from the types going in and out. It was very dark inside, and almost before I could focus, George grabbed my arm, which was quite a surprise, since I'd forgotten by then that he would be there. His little friend Daniel was there too, more or less with him—I couldn't tell which. George seemed rather nervous, a quality I had not previously associated with him. But then I hadn't seen him for a couple of years, during which time he'd left his law firm, announced to the world in general that he was queer, and raced off to Paris to prove it. We had just begun to talk, and then, suddenly, he went dashing off after some character, saying he'd explain later. Daniel and I were left standing, looking rather awkward, when you chose just that moment to make your entrance.

"Hello, sweetness!" you declaimed, reaching into your pocket. "I've brought some of that home-grown Connecticut grass." And when I seemed astonished that it would have lasted so long, you avowed that you never smoked it anymore; you had no one fun to smoke it with in Paris. With that, you thrust a joint at me, ordering, "Light it up!" Which I did, despite several protests, which you squelched in short order. You lit one too, and we both sat down and became instantly aware of the blond boy sitting next to you. He had been there all along, but we hadn't noticed before. Now we noticed. Both of us. "Do you see *that*, my dear?" you asked rhetorically, and before I'd exhaled a smoky affirmative answer, you'd already reached over and put your joint into the boy's mouth—without even so much as a "Hello," I recall. Not only did he not protest, he simply closed his eyes and inhaled.

That, I decided, was the clue for my departure, so I stood up and moved some three inches to the right. This put me in the immediate proximity of a bushy-haired, carefully costumed, hippie type, who was obviously even more stoned than I—albeit not for long. We commenced what turned into a completely unsatisfactory and lengthy conversation, which somehow seemed both amusing and profound at the time. During this period, you and the blond number, whose name was Henri, announced an immediate departure. Meanwhile, my hippie "friend" and I traded glasses. He wore my granny gold-rims off to another corner of the place, and I sat down wearing his sunglasses. This made the room even darker than it already was and isolated me completely. I decided to pretend I was blind, which was fun for a little while, until I realized that nothing happens to a blind person in a bar like that. It had become quite clear that I wasn't going to score with this number, and besides, by then I didn't want to. So I went off in search of him and my own glasses, which I eventually recovered. I ran into Daniel, en route, who thought I'd lost my mind, and I was obliged to point out that it was simply misplaced.

Having recovered both sight and equilibrium, I went back to sit at the bar and start all over. Just then, in bounced Henri with a large, blond smile. Since he was back already, it was pointless to ask if he were back already; instead, I asked if you were coming back too, and he said you were not. With a flourish, he produced one of your Connecticut joints, which we then proceeded to share, much to my delight. We discussed Japan, his Japanese lover, his ambitions to leave for Japan as soon as possible, and various other exotic subjects until it was time to leave.

Henri and I got into a taxi and went to his apartment, a top-floor walk-up near the Gare St. Lazare. We walked up incredible numbers of stairs. He opened the door, and a shiny little brown dog jumped on us with enormous and obvious happiness. Since the little beast had just peed all over the floor, I wasn't too happy to see her. Henri, however, picked her up, kissed her, cleaned the floor, and made coffee. We discussed Japan some more and finally decided to go to bed. I promised I would wake him at eight, since he said he wouldn't be able to wake up by himself; he had to catch a plane, he said, and before that, take the dog, whose name was Stéphanie, to his mother's house so that he could leave for Japan.

It was a bit difficult undressing him; Stéphanie kept get getting in the way. Henri, in fact, simply lay down on the bed, with Stéphanie kissing him and licking quite frantically. Finally I had all his clothes off, with Stéphanie now licking him all over and Henri patting her on the head, saying, "Stéphanie, arrête, arrête . . ." which was apparently an order to continue. As soon as I took off my own clothes, Stéphanie began to lick me all over, too. It occurred to me then to leave instantly, but it was too late to do anything instantly. Furthermore, both Lust and Grass had overcome my better judgment. I decided it was, after all, something new, wasn't it? So while Henri lay there quiescently, I sucked him off for a while, as Stéphanie licked both of us all over. Then, because he was so completely passive, I fucked him thoroughly, without even asking. All the while, Stéphanie was licking away madly, and when Henri came, all over my hands and his belly, she jumped right up and licked it all off. When I pulled out, she licked me off too, my cock and balls, with Henri just lying there saying, "Elle sait bien qu'elle ne doit pas faire ça."

We fell asleep fitfully and both awakened at eight. It was too early, and we were too tired to screw again, so we dressed. Henri put Stéphanie into a small satchel, and we went downstairs to the neighborhood bar for *café au lait* and a croissant. We said *"au r'voir,"* and I went back to my room, took a shower, shaved, and went off to meet Mother for breakfast.

Later in the day I called you to say thanks for a lovely evening—do you remember? You asked me if it had been successful, and I admitted it had, although nothing more. Then, brassy bitch that I am, I asked you how your trick had been, and you said, "My dear, he was too, too divine!" And not only that, you added, "He was fabulous sex."

At the time, it was too much to go into, especially over the telephone, but I knew I could not resist keeping the rest to myself. Now, of course, we're back to everyday perversions, distance hath lent enchantment, and I can with equanimity divulge *all*. May the gods preserve us!

Come and see us on your way back. We have a guestroom ready, at last. Bring Henri, Stéphanie, Larry, or anyone you want to.

Love, Angus

A Scent of Violets
1971

My mother's favorite scent was violet, and as a young child I learned to please her on birthdays or Mother's Day with perfumes and colognes such as "English Violet" and "Devon Violets," which was more foreign because it was packaged in a delicate white, porcelain jug, instead of a glass bottle. It never occurred to me to attempt to grow them, because violet was a "girly" smell and certainly not appropriate for boys.

Violets are not easy to grow, it turns out. It wasn't until I lived in Los Angeles, many years later, in a glass house on a hill halfway between downtown L.A. and Pasadena, that a tile shelf above the kitchen sink proved to be the perfect place for violets to thrive. Ever since, have I been successful in growing them.

Decades ago, when I lived in Boston with my first long-term boyfriend Eddie, a popular gay bar sat at the foot of Beacon Hill, just across from Massachusetts General Hospital. It was easily accessible by public transport and equidistant from Harvard Square and downtown. Called "Sporter's," it was a dirty, sleazy, dump of a place, run by an overweight, good-natured, Irish fellow called Bob who never seemed able to remember anyone's name.

Eddie and I lived on Pinckney Street, just off Charles, and we often dropped into Sporter's late in the evening, after a concert or a movie. After a few years we became irregular "regulars" there. Despite its ugliness, Sporter's was popular with boys from Harvard, MIT, Northeastern, Emerson, Tufts, and various other colleges and schools in the area, as well as with occasional out-of-towners, businessmen, soldiers, and sailors. I liked the variety and mix there.

I met Ted, a hunky local boy with a fetching, thick Boston accent. Every four or five months, when we were both at the bar late and hadn't met anyone new, we would end up together. Another fellow, a handsome, sexy Black man called Tom, was another memorable, occasional trick over many years.

One of my favorite Sporter's friends was Allyn, an icono-clastic artist who lived in a cold-water, walk-up flat, which I considered inconceivable in wintry New England. Allyn, a true regular at the bar, wore shoulder-length, blond hair, which he would wash occasionally, and over which he would place a white cowboy hat with a rabbit-fur band and a couple of pigeon feathers. Allyn made beautiful silverpoint drawings, with a delicacy and refinement that belied his bohemian appearance. He also had a wild side, which eventually led to his demise one summer when I was vacationing in France. The story circu-lated that he dropped a tab of LSD atop a friend's roof and decided he could fly. Before that unhappy moment, luckily, I had engaged him to paint a mural of his own design, which he entitled "Muriel," above the wainscoting in our nineteenth century dining room—a *fête champêtre* he produced in muted, sepia colors portraying fauns and nymphs disporting them-selves in sylvan groves and grottoes. Funny, sardonic, usually broke, and often drunk, I can still hear him as we walked into the bar, calling out, "Hey, guys, how about a smart *cocktail de choize?*"—which meant he wanted a fresh can of beer.

On occasion, Eddie and I would pick up a lonely fellow and take him home for fun, music, and sex, because those were the days before AIDS—before the world became suspicious and terri-fied. It was not uncommon to meet a guy, connect, and invite him home for the night—and sometimes keep him over for breakfast. In fact, over the twelve years we lived in Boston, a number of these fellows became good friends.

In addition to Sporter's, we enjoyed other popular gay hang-outs in town. The Napoleon fancied itself an upscale, darkly elegant club, with velvet walls, an upstairs bar featuring paint-ings and prints of the emperor adorning every wall and corner. Gentlemen worked in suits or tuxedos, and from time to time, even white tie and tails.

The Other Side, located in Boston's "Combat Zone," was wonderful for intrepid slumming with a dangerous, exotic and mysterious clientele. The Purple Orchid, the city's longest-running servicemen's bar, had opened during WWII and remained popular until the late seventies, when it vanished, to be replaced by a group of newer, louder, and younger discos and clubs.

Eddie liked to hang out at The Tool Box, a "leather bar" downtown near the Boston Conservatory of Music, where our friend Danny Pinkham would occasionally drop in for a beer after teaching. One day I asked him, "Danny, what would happen if you should run into one of your students here?"

Without a moment's hesitation, he answered, in his impeccable, flutey New England tones, "You can't be seen in a place you don't frequent."

I found the clientele at Sporter's more congenial, and from time to time, Eddie and I would both arrive home with a new trick in tow, in those gentler and easier times. One night, out on my own, I encountered a slim, handsome young man wearing chinos, a light blue shirt, and a dark sweater. One of his eyes was mossy green and the other light blue, and he exuded genteel charm and understated *savoir faire*. We would occasionally run into each other, and eventually I worked up the courage to ask his name and invite him home for the night. He was a dream date, with soft skin, light brown hair with red gold highlights, and a languid, intoxicating beauty. We made love and fell asleep for a while, and I awoke to the scent of violets.

Knowing there were no flowers in the room, I realized it was Bill, who was blessed with a completely natural scent of violets, which I had never experienced. We showered and shared coffee in the morning, and off he went into his day and I into mine. I can still picture him clearly in my mind's eye, and I've often dreamed of his sweet lips and unique scent of violets, hoping for another night with him. Occasionally we would meet in the bar and converse briefly. Once I ran into him downtown at midday with an older woman, whom he introduced as his aunt, and we shared a lovely lunch. After that I never saw him again, yet never forgot him or his scent of violets.

♈

The San Antonio Power Jacket

1974

A friend at dinner told me he was from San Antonio and then proceeded to tell me how boring it was there. In response, I told him it was one of the most interesting places I had ever visited. Startled and surprised, he asked me to explain, so I did, happily.

As a young art dealer living in Boston in the early seventies, I learned it was worthwhile to take business trips away from Boston in the early Spring, because there was no "early spring" in Massachusetts and winter sometimes lasted until May. Consequently, I took spring business trips to Florida, Texas, California, and somewhere else that might be warmer and nicer than Boston in February, March, or April—which was almost anywhere.

San Antonio was a particularly lovely destination with an atmospheric old hotel I liked called the St. Anthony. When you checked in at the St. Anthony, not many questions were asked, and fewer required answers.

I knew the directors of two museums in San Antonio, so it was an advantageous place for me to visit. I arrived with a portfolio of old master prints and drawings, along with a few modern works on paper, and several edgy newer works plus, startlingly at the time, photographs daring the attempt to pass as Art.

After a couple of days showing my wares around town, the work week was over, and it was time to celebrate. I took off my three-piece suit, put on a pair of jeans and a pair of Western boots, and set off toward a local bar, which I'd located in a gay guide. Because business had gone well, I was feeling flush and in an expansive mood, deciding on the spur of the moment to take a hit of MDA, which we used to call "The Pink Pill." It enhanced the evening and helped me overcome my slight nervousness about going out to a new bar in a strange town.

Arriving at the bar, called the San Antonio Country, I saw a lot of frantic activity and some unusual sort of confusion, which I didn't immediately comprehend. I bought a drink and watched what was happening for a while, and it seemed to be a rummage sale. Never having seen a rummage sale before in a gay bar, I decided to ask one of the locals what was going on. It turned out that some of the fellows frequenting the place had decided they wanted to go on a ski trip. None of them had sufficient money to rent a vehicle large enough, so they arranged to hold a rummage sale in the bar to collectively raise funds for a trip to the nearby ski region.

Amused by the concept, I wandered through the tables, looking at old shirts, old boots, magazines, and trivia which I found of little interest. In the very last row, however, a sparkling jacket hanging on a rack caught my eye. Originally a plain denim, Levi jacket, it had been lovingly tended and decorated over many years. The back bore a large letter C (for Claude, who had created this extravaganza) surrounded by jewels and a variety of artifacts. In addition, the entire front, sides, and sleeves of the jacket had been decorated, fitted out, and encumbered with a vast array of pins, buttons, attachments, brooches, and every possible piece of bad costume jewelry imaginable. The left sleeve had a row of feathers sewn on in such a way that when you were leaning on the bar, the feathers didn't get damaged. It was fabulous!

On the upper left lapel was attached a tiny bronze hand with a small clamp, grasping bits of paper. When I inquired about the purpose of the bronze hand with the small bits of paper, I was looked at askance and told, with some attitude, that the paper bits were for giving out your phone number, in case anyone asked.

By this time, the drugs had kicked in, and I was feeling ever more expansive. I asked to try on the jacket, and it fit perfectly. Obviously, it was nothing at all like any Boston jacket I'd ever worn. It weighed about thirty pounds, and because of all the jangling accoutrements, when I moved or attempted to dance, the jacket went into a rhythmic, noisy counterpoint of its own. I was totally enthralled and asked the price, which was a hundred dollars. Back then, that was more than three times the price of a brand-new Levi jacket. I contemplated the time and energy it would require to replace the adornments already in place and told Claude, the seller, that I would buy it. I vaguely recall telling him that it was an amazing piece of work, perhaps a master-piece, and that it would probably end up in a museum. (At the time, the Metropolitan Museum was enjoying great success with its newly opened fabric and costume department.)

For a half-hour or so, I wore the jacket around the bar, enjoying the weight of it and the noises it made. Unbeknownst to me at the time, news had flown around the bar like wildfire that a crazy art dealer from Boston had paid Claude a hundred dollars for his Levi jacket and was going to put it into a museum. In no time, the jacket was gathering so much attention that it made me nervous, so I took it back to Claude and asked him to put it away for a while, until I could work up to wearing it again.

After a few more drinks, I made another sashay around the bar, wearing the jacket comfortably this time, and I was cruised and approached more than at any time in my life. I quickly realized that it wasn't about me, per se, but that the jacket had its own power, which an amazing variety of men responded to in different ways. At one point, two fellows were fighting about which one was going to take me home. This was a quandary unprecedented in my experience. While I was going a little crazy trying to figure out which of these two extremely attractive guys I should choose, the door of the bar swung open, and a stunning blond cowboy wearing tight jeans and a form-fitting shirt walked in, took one look around the bar, made a beeline towards me and asked simply, "Ya wanna fuck?"

After all the pussyfooting of the previous half-hour, I had no choice. Without hesitation, I looked him in both eyes and replied in as husky a tone as I could muster, "I never have before, but I think you've talked me into it, you silver-tongued Romeo."

I scarcely had a chance to bid goodnight to the two boys who were fighting for my attentions. The cowboy grabbed my arm, almost dragged me out of the bar, and pulled me into his bright pink, slightly battered, 1955 Packard convertible, which had a cracked windshield. The whole scene was too fine to believe! And then it got better.

We drove back to the St. Anthony Hotel, ordered drinks sent up to the room, and hardly unable to rip the clothes off each other quickly enough during the first second, took a breath and realized we were in no hurry. We had the whole night, after all. The cowboy was lean and tan, incredibly hot in every possible way, and we both knew it was going to be fun, whatever "it" would be—lots of fun! We probably smoked a puff or two because it didn't matter. If we did, it was part of the ritual.

He lay down on the bed, looked up and said: "Stand in front of the mirror." So I did. Then he commanded: "Take off your boots." So I did. Slowly. Very slowly. Then, "Okay, now take off your jeans."

Having a silent moment of doubt whether I should take off my briefs along with the Levis, I threw caution to the winds, took off my jeans and briefs simultaneously, in one fluid flourish, and threw them halfway across the room. I turned, and we looked at each other deep in the eyes. I was standing there naked, except for my shirt and The Jacket. At that point, he got up and stood next to me, facing the mirror, turned towards it and said to my reflection in the mirror, "Take off my boots."

So I began, and while I was taking them off, one by one, he almost fell and grabbed my shoulder for support. Then, looking into my eyes in the mirror, said: "Now take off my jeans." So, with no further introspection, I grabbed his jeans—he wore no underwear—and pulled them down, very slowly and very gently, looking into his eyes the entire way. "Okay," he said. "Now I want you to put that jacket on me."

He was going to take my Persona. He wanted to wear it. He wanted it on his body on his skin. I was thrilled *and* flummoxed. I wanted my body on his, on his skin. But I had to wait.

"All right," I told him, "You can try it on, but you have to know, it's going to hurt."

"Why would it hurt?" he queried.

"You'll find out soon," I warned him. "All those pins and brooches and feathers and applications to the jacket have metal points and rivets inside, and they can hurt if there's enough pressure applied. It's not smooth and simple and easy. "It's a Man's Jacket," I added. "Are you man and cowboy enough?"

At that, he pulled off his blue Western shirt, which was all that was left, and devouring him with my eyes, I took off the Power Jacket, carefully, and helped him into it. His eyes sparkled almost as much as the bling on the jacket, and he didn't care if it hurt. By then, neither did I. I began to press different parts of his body, and he groaned with pleasure, as the pins pressed in. While applying pressure to different areas of The Jacket, and to his skin directly underneath, I was touching his back, his arms, his shoulders, his butt, his thighs, his legs, his calves—to every part I could reach except his cock and balls. Those, I was saving for later. It was driving us both crazy.

He knew it, of course, and every spot where I touched him became electrified. I was becoming more and more excited, as was he, and we kept up the suspense and the teasing until it simply wasn't tolerable for one more instant. I pulled the Jacket off him, and, finally, we were both naked, falling into each other's arms and chests and bellies and legs and feet and ramrod-stiff cocks, rubbing each other with gently wild and insistent pressure. The heat was intense, and it continued to increase. We were on and off each other in almost every way possible, spending the rest of the night together making such a racket that management twice had to telephone and ask us to please hold back.

It wasn't possible, however. Or repeatable.

The next morning I flew back to Boston, never saw the cowboy again, never knew his name, never again saw the pink Packard convertible, yet had one of the most unexpected, sexiest and wildest nights of my life. Up until then, at least.

Would you like to see the San Antonio Power Jacket? I'll put it on for you . . . if you're man—or woman—enough.

♈

The Heartland

1976

It began as a simple business trip to Kansas City to visit a client, Bob McDonnell, a serious art collector in his hometown, and following up for an appointment with a curator at the Nelson-Atkins Gallery of Art.

Bob very generously offered to pick me up at the airport. He did so, in a splendid Rolls-Royce, complaining that his wife didn't like for him to drive his Maserati sportscar anymore. Not feeling too sorry for him, I was nonetheless grateful—especially when he dropped me off at the Crown Plaza Hotel, which happened to be hosting the Democratic National Convention at the time.

As the Rolls pulled up to the entry, I saw an extremely tall Black man, wearing something like a Beefeater's costume, with a head-dress that made him appear at least eight feet tall. The man bent down, swept open the passenger's door, extended a hand to help me out (which I didn't need), and said in a loud, deep voice: "You don' look like no democrat to me!"—a comment to which I failed to reply. He helped me with my bag and a large portfolio of prints and drawings that I'd brought along in the airplane (back in the days when it was easy to do that).

Bob remained in the car because he weighed some three hundred pounds and never moved unless it was essential. As I exited, he said: "I'll pick you up at six-thirty this evening, and we'll be taking you to The Club for dinner. I think you'll like it, and I've reserved a table right under Tom Benton's mural."

What he didn't tell me was that he and his wife had also invited Thomas Hart Benton and his wife Rita to dinner—a most welcome surprise which he knew I would appreciate. The Club was elegant, the service unobtrusive, the steaks charred to perfection, the conversations lively, and I was delighted to meet and spend an evening with a living legend of the art world.

The following day, I hauled my portfolio over to Bob's house and showed him a selection of artworks I believed he would find of interest. He purchased a Mary Cassatt aquatint and a François Villon etching—which certainly made my trip worthwhile—and that afternoon I completed my transaction at the Gallery.

Flushed with success, I got out my guidebook to see if there was a gay bar anywhere nearby. I found one within walking distance from the hotel. It was only five o'clock in the evening, so I had no expectations, but I decided to give it a try. I felt a bit out of place in my Bostonian three-piece suit. Besides the bartender, only one other patron, a youthful boy who appeared to be barely twenty-one, was sitting at the bar.

I seated myself close by, and we talked about nothing much. The bartender turned on the sound system and was playing gentle dance music, so I asked the boy if he'd like to dance, and he accepted. We had a few chaste and distant dances, and I asked him his name. He replied, "Marilyn."

That seemed as surreal as the black doorman in the Beefeater's costume, and I truly had no idea that the boy was a lesbian, her drag and demeanor were so convincing.

The following day I flew to San Antonio, where I had appointments at the McNay Art Institute, then on to Houston for appointments with the Contemporary Museum of Art and the Fine Arts Museum. The Director of the Contemporary Museum invited me to a party that evening, which I considered a friendly and civilized gesture.

Once again, I dressed up with a new lightweight khaki suit, a white shirt and a spectacular tie, expecting everyone to be similarly dressed. Instead, a small group of artists were attending and wearing paint-spattered t-shirts. They clearly considered me The Enemy and would have nothing to say to me under any circumstances, thinking me some sort of East Coast snob, I suppose.

A bit ill at ease for a few minutes, I ordered a drink and wondered what to do to make an impression with these rude people. An elegant woman in a full-length gown, composed of tiny pieces of emerald-colored metal links, appeared suddenly and spectacularly into the room. We gravitated to each other and began a conversation, mostly centered around the artists who were concentrating far too hard on ignoring us. I remarked to her how unpleasant I was finding the event, and she agreed, so I asked if she'd like to join me in shaking up their complacency. She laughingly agreed, and I said, "Come with me," which she did, and we went into the rest room.

She asked, "What are we doing here?"

I told her, "We're going to exchange clothes, go out on the floor for one dance, and then come back here and change back. They might even notice!" Fortunately, she was thrilled with the idea, took off her emerald gown, put on my khaki suit, white shirt and spectacular tie, and looked terrific. I put on as much of the emerald gown as possible, she zipped up the back for me to about three-quarters, and we emerged onto the dance floor.

The room fell into complete silence, except for the music. We enjoyed our single dance—with her leading, of course—then returned to the restroom and changed back into our own outfits.

Our ploy was successful. The Director was vastly amused, and the artists began to warm up and accept us as real people. The woman was obliged to leave for a dinner engagement and apologized, unnecessarily, for her early departure, telling me what a wonderful time she'd had and how she wished her husband had been there. I agreed that it had been a wonderful time, and just then learning that she was a Trustee of the Museum, I expressed my gratitude that her husband had not been there, or it would never have happened.

Martina & Shirley
1977

If you're a gay man, you know a lot of opera queens, and even if you're not, you may nonetheless have read about them. They're the fellows who attend every performance of every opera, know most of the arias and libretti by heart, and who maintain strong opinions about the vocal qualities, strengths, weaknesses, eccentricities, sexual peccadilloes, stories, and anecdotes about every performer.

In Manhattan, where I lived in the late seventies, my business partner, Mendy Wager, was a Big Opera Queen—or perhaps an Empress. He was also the voiceover king of New York City, one of the few opera queens who was also the King of something. Mendy was the voice of Dodge, the voice of Carnegie Hall (because he could speak five languages and pronounce everything perfectly) and, because he enjoyed an innate, brilliant gift for timing and timbre, was also the voice of Drano—less glamorous but more lucrative. His commercial for Drano made him famous and the product sexy.

Lenny Bernstein, a neighbor in the Dakota and great friend of Mendy's, often wrote and gave him spoken parts, not only for performances of his own compositions, such as the Kaddish, Symphony Number 3, but for others as well. Following one performance in New York of Stravinsky's "A Soldier's Tale," which Lenny conducted and for which Mendy performed the spoken narrative, the reviewer for the *New York Times* wrote the next day, "The venerable Mr. Wager has a circus in his throat."

Terrence McNally, also a Big Opera Queen and one of Mendy's best friends, wrote a play modeled on Mendy, The *Lisbon Traviata,* about a pirated recording of a Maria Callas performance in Lisbon. The main character of the play was named "Mendy," which was appropriate because Terrence appropriated Mendy's flamboyance, comments, inflections, opinions, and mannerisms as his template for the character. Some ten years after the play was written and about to be cast for the first time, Mendy was very excited, understandably, because he assumed that he would be cast in "his" role for the performance. Instead, he was informed by Terrence that he was "too old to play himself," which not only offended him, but broke his heart. Their long-time friendship ended abruptly at that point, although the play went on to great success.

A well-known story was then making the rounds of Manhattan about Martina Arroyo and Shirley Verrett, artists who had both been invited to Cairo in 1974 to perform in the hundredth anniversary of the first performance of *Aîda*, composed by Verdi in honor of the opening of the Suez Canal. Acclaimed grand ladies of the Metropolitan Opera, Arroyo and Verrett had worked and performed together despite their differences in character and style. Martina remained friendly and down-to-earth, while Shirley was known to have taken on a few airs—as befits a diva.

Upon arrival in Cairo, they were invited for a tour of the city and neighboring monuments, historical sites, and countryside. As their limousine passed through vast fields of plants and blossoms, Shirley asked in flutey tones, "What is the name of that lovely blue flower?"

Martina glanced at her askance and replied: "Honey, dat is cot-ton!"

Shortly thereafter, I was introduced to Martina at a party, recounted the story, and asked if she had really said that. She threw back her head, laughed and replied heartily, "Not exactly. What I said to her was, 'Honey, dat is cot-ton, and you used to *pick it!*'"

The Ketamine Trip
1978

Like most of my friends and peers in the late 1960s and early 1970s, I learned to expand my mind—a good idea at the time.

I had avoided marijuana for a long time, but when I finally experienced the delights, sensations, relaxation, and realizations of its benefits, I gave up my negative attitude about drugs. It wasn't too difficult because I had grown up with drugstores on every street corner. Everyone had. We went to drugstores for sandwiches, cokes, phosphates, root-beer floats, ice-cream sodas, and milkshakes. It was early preparation for better things, but we didn't know it at the time.

My first "real" drug trip happened in Boston, in 1968. I was feeling sick, with nasty cold symptoms about to explode into the whole thing. A friend came over and suggested we take a hit of mescaline. I was wearing about six layers of sweaters and feeling chills, so I said, "Sure, it couldn't be any worse than this."

The mescaline trip was brilliant—full of lights and colors, hallucinations, and other-worldliness—all sorts of experiences and feelings, new and different. When I awoke the following morning, I felt rejuvenated and wonderful, having determined that mescaline was a cure for the common cold.

A few years later, with great good luck, on the eve of a vacation trip to the Caribbean, another friend gave me and my boyfriend, Eddie, two rather large pink pills, suggesting we find a nice beach and try them out. We had booked a flight to San Juan, Puerto Rico, and neither of us had ever been there before. We spent a couple of days in San Juan, then rented a car to drive around the island. It was always in the back of my mind that we needed to find a place on a quiet, private beach, and for the first two days, that didn't happen.

On the third day, we came upon a small resort called Rincon. It was run by an elderly couple who had left Germany far behind and established a little corner of Paradise with about a half-dozen small cabins on a perfect beach, the entire place filled with exotic birds and complete privacy. It seemed perfect.

We unpacked quickly, made a run to the nearest market, and filled our shopping bags with staples—fruits, rum, fruit juices, and sweet things—because we assumed we'd have the munchies, sooner or later. Once provisioned and settled, with everything put away properly, we put on our swimsuits, gathered our towels, sunscreen, and prepared for the beach, which was only a few steps away. I opened a bottle of pineapple juice and said, "Let's take those pills before we go."

Eddie, asked somewhat reluctantly, "Now?"

I told him, "We've been driving around for days looking for the perfect beach, and we've found it. *Yes,* now! It's time!" We took the pink pills with the pineapple juice, picked up our beach gear, and opened the door. What we encountered was a white peacock, preening its tail, on the staircase. It was truly spectacular. I took a step backward and said: "Do you think those pills have started already?"

Eddie said, "I think it's too soon. That looks like a real peacock." And so it was. I took a photo of it to be certain.

We proceeded to the beach, which was deserted, beautiful, and a wondrous antidote to a New England winter. We arranged the towels and took a little walk.

Eddie said, "I don't feel very well."

I replied, "Let's just sit down here and look at these blossoms." An enormous hibiscus tree was loaded with intense red blossoms. We sat down under the tree, examining the blossoms as if we had never seen one before. And, in fact, we had never seen any like that. The brilliance of the scarlet leaves, the bright yellow of the stamens, the warmth of the sun, the concentration on the hibiscus flowers, and the intensities of the drug removed all that discomfort within moments.

We settled into a sense of bliss as novel as it was delicious. We talked about anything and everything. We had no boundaries, no right or wrong. It was All Good. We took a walk along the beach, swam in the warm sea, and melted into a comfort zone that was conscious, articulate, comfortable, and exquisite in every way. Time ceased to exist, and we spent the entire afternoon on the beach, with never a thought of food or music or anything else but the profound experience of Now . . . no judgments, opinions, or attitudes. It was perfect.

We remained there to watch the sunset and eventually returned to our cabin, where for some strange reason we weren't hungry or anxious for dinner. We fixed pineapple and rum drinks and went to bed, where we had lots of fun because we were too wired to sleep.

When we returned home to Boston, we learned that the pink pill was called MDA, and it was fabulous, according to everyone with whom we discussed it. No one disagreed about that at all.

During the next few years, I purchased large quantities of it because I feared it was too good to remain available. My fears were realized, and it was subsequently declared dangerous and illegal. Meanwhile, I had the good fortune to share it with all the friends I knew and trusted. No one ever a negative reaction to it. The truth was that MDA had been developed as an appetite depressant, and it was prescribed for overweight people who wished to change their bodies. What happened was that they felt so good on MDA, they didn't care if they were overweight or not. They felt happy, connected, loving, and wonderful. These reactions were called "unpleasant side effects" by the Powers That Were. The rest of us called MDA "The Love Drug."

In Fall of 1978 I took a trip to California with my friend Addison Lee, and we were invited to visit his college roommate, Don Donegan, who was working at Wildwood Retreat, above the Russian River, in Cazadero. The retreat was between bookings, and no one was there but Don, so we had the entire 220 acres to ourselves. We hiked and relaxed, lay in the sun and swam in the pool. Although Don and Addison had been friends for years, it was the first time he and I had met. On the second or third day there, we are all lying by the pool, and Don asked, "Do you trust me?"

I thought it was a curious question, and I asked him why he was inquiring. He replied, "You'll find out. Just tell me if you really trust me."

I said, "Of course."

"In that case," he continued, "stand on the concrete next to the pool." I did that, and he stood behind me, and commanded, "Now just fall backwards, and I'll catch you." Without hesitation, I fell backwards, and he caught me. Then he added, "You really do trust me, don't you?"

I said, "Of course. You're one of Addison's best friends, therefore you must be trustworthy. Now tell me why we engaged in this exercise."

He looked around, as if to see if someone might be listening, but no one was there but us. Still, he lowered his voice and told us, "I've been working with a mentor called Oscar Ichazo, and he's introduced me to ketamine. Have you heard of it?"

I told him I'd read books and articles by John Lilly, who had been experimenting with the drug repeatedly over time, but I had never tried it." He continued: "I have access to pure ketamine, and if you both would like to try it, I'm willing to share it with you." Intrigued by the idea, the beauty of the setting, warmth of the sunshine, and the privacy of the retreat, both of us agreed to try it. Don then explained that we could not do it all together like marijuana or hash; it was not a social drug nor a long-acting drug. It was a solitary experience; our minds would depart from our bodies, so one of us at a time would do it and the other two would remain. They would take care of the earthbound body of the one tripping until the mind returned from its voyage. He also told us it was not a pill or a tab, but an injection, which made me nervous. Injected drugs did not have a good reputation, as far as I knew. He assured us he had considerable experience and that we need not worry, and I believed him.

I took my big towel, spread it out next to the pool and lay down. Addison sat on one side and Don sat on the other. It was quiet and comfortable, and I was not afraid. Don gave me the injection in my arm, quite professionally, and it didn't hurt. Then, within moments, my body relaxed completely, and I felt my mind leaving. It went straight up into the sky, and I could look down, see the pool, my supine body, and my two friends flanking it, as my mind moved ever upward rapidly, through various layers of clouds and atmospheres. Shortly, I felt the presence of other beings who were contacting me wordlessly. I could hear and understand them, without words, which was a novel experience. They were tall and slender, not humanoid, but rather angular and crystalline, as if made of silver and titanium. Their presence was calm, all-knowing, and reassuring.

I felt no fear as they escorted me higher and higher into the stratosphere, and gradually I felt or heard a murmuring sound in the distance, which soon became a humming noise. We approached what first appeared to be a river, then a moebius strip, composed of souls, twisting and turning, some almost swimming, some jumping in, some exiting, all calmly, quietly, and elegantly. I believed all these souls were eternal; they could enter and depart this exalted state, apparently, whenever they wished or chose, and return when it was time for them to do so. In between, they dwelt in other realms, presumably on earth, perhaps elsewhere. I felt I had been awarded a glimpse into a world of eternity, where death was not a fearful state, but a quiescent place between incarnations or stations. I realized that death was nothing to fear, but another form of existence, and reveled in this knowledge which had been given to me. The silver and crystalline beings, still wordlessly, let me know when it was time to leave and escorted me silently back down through the stratosphere, atmosphere, past clouds and crystalline mountains, until I could see first the earth and the oceans, then the continents, North America, California, and back to where I began, where my body was still lying on the towel next to the pool. They escorted me sweetly, slowly, and quietly back into my body, and I could feel it return into its usual place, gently, a little at a time.

As consciousness returned, I felt a bit groggy for a few minutes, and lay there thinking about what had just happened. The fellows helped me up, and I sat in a chair for a while, collecting my thoughts. It seemed as if I had been away for a long, long time, and when I asked how long it had been, they told me about twenty-five minutes, which was hard to believe, given all I had seen, felt, and experienced.

And these many years later, I remember clearly what I saw, experienced and felt. It was truly extraordinary.

Dinner at the White House
1978

During my early visits to Washington, D.C., in the late '60s and throughout the '70s on business trips, I visited all the museums: the Phillips, the National Gallery, the National Portrait Gallery, the Building Museum, the Hirschhorn, the Smithsonian, the East Wing, the Craft Museum, and the Freer Gallery. When a friend asked if I had visited the White House, I replied: "No."

"Why not?" he asked, adding, "There are tours, you know."

I replied, "I'm not going to the White House until I'm invited."

Then it happened. In 1978, I was helping Leonard Bernstein during the summer months and dating John Browning, whom I had met through Sam Barber. Sam had composed his brilliant piano concerto specifically for John to play.

John was intense, sexy, and a superb pianist with the most beautiful piano I'd ever seen or heard: a fruitwood Hamburg Steinway from 1937, which he had recently acquired. It had almost never been played or used. In exquisite condition, the action, the tone, the ease of playing it were extraordinary, and I loved hearing him play the Rachmaninoff etudes in his spacious apartment—an upper East Side, glass high-rise.

Lenny and Sam had been invited to the very first Kennedy Center Awards. They invited John and me to join them for the dinner event at the White House, as well as for the subsequent concert and awards ceremony.

John had a drinking problem. It didn't seem to affect his playing, but it did affect his personality. I disliked being near him when he'd drunk too much Scotch. Of course I wanted to attend the event at the White House, and I wanted to go with him if he promised to not get drunk. He promised.

At Saks Fifth Avenue I bought a new tuxedo—a three-piece Valentino, which fit perfectly. The vest accommodated my nineteenth century pocket watch, its gold chain, and amethyst fob. Not surprisingly, I wanted to make a good impression.

The flight from New York to Washington was uneventful, and we checked in at the Watergate Hotel with plenty of time to get ready. Lenny had a suite, and Sam had his own room, while John, and I were in a double. We had a good time settling in and dressing up, and as we left the hotel, it began to rain.

Hoping the weather wouldn't put a damper on the proceedings, we took a taxi to the White House, entered through a reception line where we met Jimmy and Rosalyn Carter. I was surprised that Rosalyn's handshake was firmer than Jimmy's, but it didn't matter because it was such a delight to have the opportunity to see all the improvements Jackie Kennedy had made to the interiors. We strolled through the building, down the elegant hallways now crammed with cables, cords, lighting enhancements, security guards, and photographers with cameras and flash attachments constantly popping.

Following cocktails, a grand buffet dinner was served— with California wines only, which I thought was a particularly nice touch. Delicious as the dinner was, I realized halfway through that John was already drinking too much, which made me nervous. Luckily, I was seated on the opposite side of the table, adjacent to Artur Rubenstein, a great artist and one of my heroes, with his handsome son John (then appearing in the musical *Pippin*) on the other side. It was a dream come true.

The dream, sadly, turned into a nightmare. John got stinking drunk, had to be dragged back to the hotel in the rain, then he passed out. I was embarrassed, disappointed, and angry. I was outraged. Even worse, in the middle of the night, the phone rang, and the police informed us that Sam had gone missing and did we have any idea where he was. No one had any idea, and the City was combed, searching for America's composer emeritus during the wee hours with no results.

The following day we discovered Sam had gotten bored at the concert and returned to the hotel early. He went to his room, the key didn't function, and he asked a chamber maid to open the door for him. Then he lay down on the bed and went promptly to sleep, fully dressed. It turned out it wasn't his room at all, but it was unoccupied, and no one discovered him until the following morning.

That was my last date with John, and now John, Lenny, Sam, and Rubenstein have all passed on. I'm still here and happily wear the tuxedo more than thirty-five years later—and it still fits.

Sadly, or maybe not, I haven't been invited to the White House since.

The Toreador Song

for Addison Woolcott Lee, IV, in memoriam
1980

It was in New York City at the close of 1980—during the period Leonard Bernstein was regularly conducting the Vienna Philharmonic—that Mendy Wager and I gave a New Year's party in our enormous loft on Fifth Avenue for Lenny and the entire orchestra, plus choir and soloists. They had just performed Beethoven's Ninth Symphony at Avery Fisher Hall. At one point in the evening, Lenny remarked to me, in a heavy, lugubrious, mock Viennese accent, with that inimitable, gravelly, low-voice register cultivated during decades of late nights, whisky, and cigarettes, "You know, Liebchen, Vienna never was what it used to be."

I laughed in whole-hearted agreement, remembering my own discovery of that very particular, specific, universal truth.

In August of 1963, I left California with a year-long grant from University of California, Berkeley to study harpsichord and baroque music with Gustav Leonhardt at the Amsterdam Conservatory of Music. It was a fabulous and rewarding experience on every level: musical, educational, social, and sexual. Toward the close of the academic year, Leonhardt suggested that I spend the following summer at the Mozarteum Academy in Salzburg, and prepare, at the same time, for a competition in Germany. I applied for and subsequently received an extension of my U.C. grant and went off to Salzburg at the beginning of Summer, 1964. What happened then seemed simply to be Real Life, and now, reflecting on those times almost thirty years later, it seems more like a novel I read, or something that happened to someone else.

From Amsterdam I traveled by train to Salzburg, stopping in Heidelberg to call on Rainer Schütze, who was in the process of building a harpsichord I had commissioned the previous fall.

To pay for it, I'd borrowed money from my mother, who had wired funds, and I arrived at Schütze's workshop with payment in full.

The man had never seen so much cash at one time. Before he would even show me the instrument, we first had to take the money to the bank because it made him too nervous. Then I was shown only the case, the interior framing of the instrument, and the soundboard because the keyboards and strings had not yet been added. We discussed finishing details, keyboards, and scaling, and we settled on a delivery date in September, then went off to dinner. The trip had begun well, and I was excited.

Once I arrived in Salzburg, I learned that academy administrators took it upon themselves to find lodgings for students in private homes for the duration of the summer program. I was assigned an address and sent to a small, impeccably maintained house within walking distance of the academy.

Plump and proper, the proprietress was charming and friendly, and she expressed her love of music and musicians. She welcomed me with coffee and a slice of her own version of Sachertorte. Afterward, she showed me to a double room fitted with twin beds, explaining I would share the room with another music student, Michael Radulescu, a Romanian organist, due to arrive later in the day.

After unpacking, I went out to buy a bottle of Slivovitz, the delicious plum flavored Austrian liqueur, to keep on hand for late night refreshment, which, it turned out a few hours later, shocked Michael. A superb organist, the child of a German mother and Romanian father, he dwelt in a state of constant terror from having grown up in Romania. I tried to lighten him up occasionally, but it was an overwhelming task. He was brought up to believe a sip of Slivovitz was naughty, if not indeed the draught of the devil. A week or two later he would come to wonder why I seldom returned to the room to sleep. He couldn't *imagine* where I might go or what I could possibly do all night. And if he was shocked by a little bottle of Slivovitz, clearly, he wasn't ready to be told—and I certainly wasn't ready to explain it to him.

Salzburg itself was relentlessly charming. Not only was it still Mozart's town in every respect; its inhabitants continued to dress as if playing parts in an operetta. It had never occurred to me previously that Austrians, in the late twentieth century, might continue to wear dirndls and lederhosen, but they did. And they weren't costumes; they were everyday clothing. When the weather was warm, the women were startlingly voluptuous and appealing in their revealing laced bodices and décolleté. When it was cool, both men and women wore Loden coats and Tyrolian hats adorned with brushes and feathers. Furthermore, because it rained almost daily, everyone carried an umbrella—yet another theatrical prop enhancing the general operatic demeanor of the city.

Coffeehouses were traditional, lively, crowded places, and I liked sitting where Mozart might have sat to drink coffee and compose. It was also a thrill to visit Mozart's house and play on one of his pianos, a perk accorded only to students of baroque music. Classes at the Academy were simultaneously relaxed and intense, a duality which helped decipher some of the disparities of the Austrian character.

It was summertime, the Salzburg Festival was in its early days, and the ambience of the city was exciting. With student colleagues—other young musicians like myself occupied or preoccupied with Baroque music—I performed in small ensembles and set about practicing for concerts in neighboring churches and castles. Orchestral students formed a symphony and worked on separate repertoires in different styles. It was a kind of Old European dreamland for me, visually, historically, and musically.

Sometime during my first week, I met Frank Born, an American in town for the summer. In his early forties, Frank was a doctor suffering from a slight heart problem. Consequently, he had taken early retirement form Aramco Hospital, the American-Arabian medical program in Saudi Arabia, which he had helped to found. An exotic and enigmatic character, Frank maintained a house in Thailand as well as a farm in Puerto Rico. At both locations he grew extremely hot chili peppers. For a man of mild manners and delicate health, it seemed odd that he was so inordinately fond of hot peppers. The tiny peppers from Thailand, which he enjoyed offering his guests, were the hottest in the world, he claimed, smiling genially. Tall, lean, and handsome, Frank did everything slowly, so as not to disturb the delicate equilibrium of his heart. He walked and talked slowly, he dined slowly, and he made love slowly. He was elegant, well-dressed, and worldly, as well as gentle, good-natured, and sweet, and I loved him and his presence.

He in turn enjoyed my youth, musicality, enthusiasm, and relentless energy. We dated regularly all summer. He did not interfere in my music making, and I seldom saw him during the day, when I attended classes and practiced. Our rendezvous were romantic and nocturnal. Frank appreciated the Good Life and possessed the means and style to achieve as well as share it. He invited me to dinners at the Goldener Hirsch Hotel, to late suppers at cafés along the river, to concerts, the opera, and sometimes home to bed.

Frank shared a lively and popular house with André Mattoni, an Austrian baron who was then Intendant of the Vienna Opera and Herbert von Karajan's major domo and right-hand man. Frank and André were longtime friends who also owned a house together in Rome. Both men traveled frequently and were seldom in residence at the same time. The Salzburg house where they summered was charming, unpretentious, and lovely. Frank and André each had private wings; common spaces included a comfortable salon, dining room, kitchen and garden. Additional guest rooms were constantly occupied, and a cook as well as a housekeeper were on hand to take care of everyone. Visitors were legion.

The house rang with music, talk, excitement, and business, and it buzzed with an undercurrent of sexual energy. It was a wonderful place to be, and I spent as much time there as possible. Because of André and his influence, Frank could always obtain tickets to the opera. In addition, for myself and other musical friends, we had free entrée to rehearsals, which

I found particularly exciting because they were so much more personal than performances.

During that summer I incidentally met a prince—not socially, but on the street. He was the genuine article—a horny, young, aristocratic Aryan, who happened also to be blond, slender, blue-eyed, and a delight to behold. Our eyes locked, we spoke, and within moments of our meeting he had sneaked me into his father's castle. It wasn't too difficult because his father was extremely hard of hearing. We made love—as energetic as it was forbidden—in his stone bedroom, following which he sneaked me out, a procedure we repeated on several summer afternoons.

With him, everything was the opposite of anything with Frank. Sex was always in the daytime, never at night, and it was always surreptitious. Occasionally I would see the prince out in the evening, practicing the ritual Salzburg promenade with a girl on his arm. On those occasions, he would neither say hello nor acknowledge my presence in any way. As a democratic American, this annoyed me, and in those days the term "in the closet" had not yet been coined. I understood the concept without knowing the term, and I decided it was *his* problem, not mine. It didn't interfere with our occasional fervent matinées, short-lived though they were. I had early on become accustomed to double, or even triple, lives.

Late in the summer a handsome and magnetic houseguest, Robert Kerns, arrived to stay with André. A baritone with the opera in Vienna, we felt an instant mutual attraction which I briefly mistook for love at first sight. To jump into bed the first thing, however, would not have been appropriate behavior, and neither of us wished to embarrass ourselves or our hosts.

Later, Bob asked what I planned for the end of the summer and invited me to visit him in Vienna for a week. Since I had no other plans, I accepted his invitation with alacrity. Frank was moving to Puerto Rico, André was closing the Salzburg house, and Bob's offer was too fine an opportunity to forego before heading back to the U.S. I could hardly wait for the final week of classes at the Academy to end.

Bob met me at the train terminal in Vienna. Attired in Lederhosen, suspenders, and a tight polo shirt, he was so appealing I could hardly keep my hands off him. It was an effort, I recall, to remain seemly. First off, he took me in his Volkswagen for a sight-seeing drive along the Danube, which, unlike the famous waltz, was neither beautiful nor blue. He casually informed me he was to sing the role of Escamillo in *Carmen* at the Opera House that very night, and he said he'd already procured a box seat for me.

My first day in Vienna served as a rousing overture to a remarkably operatic week. As we drove along the river, I said something to the effect of, "I've never been in a car with a live opera singer. Will you sing something for me?"

With no hesitation, still driving, he opened his mouth and sang a Mozart aria. The sound and volume of his voice was so present, so forceful, so dazzling, I was overcome and shouted, "Stop! Pull off the road." As soon as the car was stopped, I undid the buttons on his Lederhosen and gave him a blowjob right then and there, in the car, at the edge of the Vienna Woods. He was as startled by the sudden blowjob as I was by the sudden aria. Of course, we'd both been waiting for the right moment since we first met.

Sitting in the box that night, watching Robert onstage, hearing him sing the "Toreador Song," remembering the afternoon drive and the blowjob—I could scarcely believe it was happening. At one point, our eyes met, and he sang directly to me. It was a sensation that I imagine would be like being hit with a bolt of lightning. Not enough of an opera queen to imagine I was Carmen (although it occurred to me later I might have considered the possibility), it was quite enough just as it was, having Escamillo serenade me from the stage of the Vienna Opera House.

Following the performance, an elegant reception and party was held in a baroque hall. I felt overwhelmed, drank too much, and excused myself to throw up in the men's room. The reception was crowded, so no one seemed to notice my brief absence.

Although I was embarrassed, I recovered rapidly since there was no time to waste. During the next four days, we strolled around Vienna, visited museums, drove to the lovely monastery at Melk, dined in Austro-Hungarian splendor at Demel's and at the Hotel Sacher, talked music, love, and life in romantic cafés, and spent glorious nights in bed together. Bob finally told me he had a lover, an Italian tenor, and that this week was an interlude for him, nothing more. When it was over he wouldn't be able to see me again, write, or even receive letters.

I realized that everything about this visit was operatic, if not tragic. It became clear that I had starred, or at least performed, in a very personal version of *Carmen*. Instead of the title role, I realized, reflecting on the situation with some remove, I had been rather suddenly demoted. Clearly, this was a Viennese riff on Bizet's opera!

So it was in New York City, at the close of 1980, when he was regularly conducting the Vienna Philharmonic, that Mendy Wager and I gave a New Year's party at our loft for Leonard Bernstein and the entire orchestra, plus choir and soloists, following a performance of Beethoven's Ninth Symphony at Avery Fisher Hall. That night Lenny made his famous remark, in his inimitable lowest register, with that lugubrious, mock-Viennese accent.

Enough time having intervened, I was able finally to laugh with sweet nostalgia, mentally hearing the Toreador Song echo through that bizarre, operatic, Viennese corrida of my memory. I comprehended completely how Vienna, indeed, never was what it used to be.

The Hitchhiker's Baby

1982

Late for a dinner party, I was rushing. To make it worse, the event was to be held way up in the Hollywood Hills, in unfamiliar territory.

I dressed in a hurry, left, and proceeded toward the Hollywood Freeway from Beachwood Canyon. At the Gower Street entrance to the Freeway, I couldn't help but notice a guy hitchhiking. I was planning to go only one stop and didn't pick him up. As I passed him, however, something made me change my mind. He was not an ordinary hitchhiker. He was tall, blond, and clean. He had a well-trimmed moustache and was carrying a suit bag and a bowling bag. I guess it was the suit bag which stopped me, as it was so unexpected.

I backed up, rolled down the car window, and asked where he was going.

He told me to Colfax and Riverside. Not knowing where that was, I said, "I'll take you to the Barham entrance to the Freeway and drop you there."

As he got into the car, he almost fell, making excuses about a heart condition and a long trip—but I could tell he was drunk. Not a little, but completely plastered. He told me, "My wife's having a baby, and I've got to go home." He seemed to be having some trouble talking. Then he told me: "I'll give you twenty dollars if you'll take me home, sir."

I asked him, "If you have twenty dollars, why didn't you take a cab from Hollywood?"

He was offended and said, "I'm a liberated man, and I don't take taxis."

That was too much drunken logic to argue with, so I didn't. He said, "They got me drunk after work. I must smell like a brewery."

"No," I said, "like a saloon." He didn't get the distinction, or even laugh, so I realized he didn't know the difference. Then I decided I was being unkind. After all, he was blond and tall and handsome—probably about twenty-four.

He thought about the saloon remark and asked, "Do I really smell?"

I replied: "I cannot tell a lie. You *reek*."

"It was Bristol Creams," he told me. "After work they got me drunk on Bristol Creams and Scotch." Then he lifted the bowling bag, announcing, "That's what's in here: Bristol Cream and Scotch. I have a cigar. It's a beautiful thing to have a child," he added. "They paged me at Blanche's. Do you know Blanche's?"

"Sure," I said. "It's a neighborhood gay bar on Bronson."

"They paged me there," he repeated, "and told me, 'Get home, your wife is having a baby!' Here," he added, holding it out towards me, "don't you want a cigar?"

"No thanks," I replied. "I don't smoke."

"Well then," he asked, "do you want a blowjob?"

I replied, "Your wife might not approve."

"She'll never know," he said. "She's in the hospital."

I was tempted, I admit, but I was running late, and he was too drunk. So I laughed, maybe a bit nervously. "You're quite a character," I remarked, "what's your name?"

"Jim," he told me, and we shook hands. By now I was fifteen minutes later for dinner, and we were approaching his corner. "Just let me out here," he said, so I pulled over. "Now, how much shall I give you, sir?" he asked.

"Nothing," I said. "I don't want you to pay me." He appeared quite shocked and thought about it seriously for a long minute. Then he looked at me carefully, decided I meant it about not wanting to be paid, and asked, "Can I give you a kiss?"

"Sure," I replied, "what a great idea!" He then gave me a terrific kiss on the lips and said, "I forgot I smell like a brewery." He pulled his suit bag and bowling bag together and got out of the car, kicking the door shut.

I was annoyed that he kicked the door, but in truth, his hands were both full. Quite full!

One of these days soon, I intend to have a drink at Blanche's and take along some baby clothes.

A Visit with Aunt El
1988

Before arriving in Los Angeles, or "El Lay" as I prefer to call it, I telephone my Aunt Leona to let her know of my impending visit. I suggest lunch on Friday, following my morning appointments, and she cheerfully agrees. I also tell her I will invite her to whichever restaurant she chooses, hoping beyond hope that she won't offer to cook.

Aunt El is now eighty-three years old, a white-haired wisp of a woman, who probably doesn't weigh more than ninety pounds. She lives alone in the house she and my Uncle Abie built more than forty years ago in the Hollywood Hills. Abie died seven years ago, and Aunt El, although her eyesight has diminished to the point where she can no longer drive, is otherwise as independent and feisty as many people half her age. Having followed regimes of low-fat, low-cholesterol, and low-taste for more than half a century, her cuisine—while original—is often bizarre. Everything's salt-free, chewy, and replete with oats, nuts, yoghurts, and substitutions for original ingredients in a variety of recipes— none of which is recognizable by the time she has created her own brand of magic. Two classic exceptions are her meringues and biscotti, which are as legendary as her eccentricities.

Irreverent, humorous, bizarre, and completely outspoken, Aunt El has always been appealing. Wit, intelligence, and musical ability are her gods, not money, social position, or notoriety. She has never dressed, thought, or behaved as anyone else, and her iconoclasm has always appealed to me.

Recently, however, the wit and charm have become partially replaced by age, indecision, impaired vision, and fear. The hardest part for me is that she has become suspicious almost to the point of paranoia and doesn't trust anyone at all, myself included. As promised, I arrive at her door shortly before noon. She meets me in her usual outfit: white sweatpants, white sweatshirt, and white tennis shoes. The ensemble crowned by her mane of white hair, she looks like a gnome of the snows or some equally improbable ice-encrusted creature invented by cinematographic imagineering.

"My love," she greets me, effusively as only a true, practiced, Old Hollywood hostess can manage, with a mixture of genuine affection and enthusiasm masked by equally effusive phoniness. "My darling, you're gorgeous as ever!" she adds.

Meanwhile, at the back of the entrance hallway, an exceedingly handsome young fellow is engaged in rewiring several electrical fixtures, and, giving his behind a familiar swat with her well-practiced hand, she introduces us, in her fashion. "This is Luke," she announces. "I fell in love with him when he was fourteen, when his father first brought him over to help. Isn't he gorgeous?"

As is usual with Aunt El, the questions are rhetorical, and it matters little whether one responds or not. Yes, Luke is gorgeous, and she knows it, and I suspect Luke knows it as well. It doesn't matter whether I acknowledge the question or not. She natters on, and her running chatter is less a dialogue and more a monologue. I have the feeling it's constant, whether anyone else is present or not.

"So," she asks, without pausing for an answer, "what are you up to?" and grabs my arm to drag me into the garden to demonstrate its sorry state, neither caring for nor expecting a response to her question. "It's the deer," she snarls, "the crummy bastards! They've eaten everything. Every stalk, every peach, every tomato. Everything but the lemons. Gawd! What's the matter with them, anyway? Why do you think they don't like lemons?"

And before she answers herself, a small Dachshund appears, carrying a stone in his mouth, almost as heavy as the dog himself, which he drops in a patch of geraniums. "Winston," she screams, "get out of the garden, you little creep!" And to me, "You remember Winston, don't you? I got him right after Abie died, but he was too much for me to handle. He kept running away." (I thought "Who could blame him?" but held my tongue.)

She continued, in her own train of ineffable logic, "I was afraid he'd get run over, so I gave him to Luke. Now Luke and his wife are divorced."

"Is that on account of Winston?" I inquire innocently.

"Of course not," she snaps, continuing "I can't imagine why they're divorced. But it doesn't really matter since they're still seeing each other. Barbara's a doll. I adore her."

Winston picks up the stone and brings it appealingly for Aunt El to throw, as though it were a stick. Then he jumps up on a ledge and knocks over a flowerpot, scattering soil and broken geraniums all over the terrace. "Give me a broom and I'll clean it up," I tell her.

"I can't," she replies. "Luke's truck is in front of the garage, so I can't open the door, and the brooms are all in the garage. Just leave it for later."

"So how much time do you have?" she inquires, as if she didn't have an agenda. I know better, of course, because she greets everyone as a potential chauffeur now that she can no longer drive. Also, as a quintessential Gemini, her behavior wavers between presumably innocent, unacknowledged passive aggression, and pure, deliberate, unadulterated manipulation.

"My next appointment is at three," I tell her, "so you have me until two-thirty." Then I ask, "Where would you like to go for lunch?"

In response she farts loudly, a trumpet call which neither of us acknowledges, and explains, in addition, that she can't possibly leave the house. There's too much going on, she can't leave Luke, and she's expecting some important telephone calls.

I protest, saying, "I thought we'd agreed I would take you wherever you'd like to go for lunch."

"Tell me what you think of this," she commands, changing the subject abruptly, as usual, and pointing towards a variety of fabric swatches arrayed over the couch. "I'm going to have the floors redone, and while that's happening, I want the couch recovered at the same time," she announces.

"Why don't you just get a new one?" I ask, knowing that

she inherited a considerable sum of money earlier this year, and that she can afford anything she wants. "I like the old one," she says, "and I'm thinking of a velvet, sort of taupe. What do you think? You have such good taste!"

I know it's a mistake, but it's true and I can't help answering, falling right into her trap. "It's not practical," I tell her. "Someone is sure to spill things on the couch, and one glass of red wine is disaster on taupe velvet."

Pensively, she remarks, "You're so practical." Then, an instant later, "You're *too* practical." She continues, "I think a really fine quality velvet will be exactly right."

"I don't know why you ever ask me anything," I counter, "because you already know exactly what you want. Why don't you just go ahead and get it?"

"But I *want* your opinion," she lies, adding, "How do you like my new rug?"

Once more, like a dope, I swallow the bait. "It's ugly," I tell her. "Too small for the room, drab and monotonous. Why didn't you get an oriental with some color?"

"Because I like it," she counters proudly, "and I want the sofa to go with it."

Changing tack once again, like a rudderless sailboat, she announces, "Now I'm going to fix us a little lunch."

Plaintively, I plead, "It's too much trouble, Aunt El. Please let me take you out."

"Nonsense," she responds. "It's no trouble at all," she says, and begins preparing lunch, whether I like it or not—which I don't.

She takes a couple of English muffins and splits them with a peculiar English muffin-splitting device housed in a sort of fabric cozy. Because the muffins are already pre-split, the device is unnecessary, but she uses it anyway, afterwards replacing it in its container. She spreads something that looks like chili sauce on the muffins, remarking, "This will make your anus quiver," then adds a layer of cheese and puts the muffins in the oven.

My heart sinks, but I tell myself she's eighty-three and that it's my duty to humor her as gracefully as possible. Not an easy task these days, and not as much fun as it used to be. Then she heats up some soup. Pea soup she had prepared earlier, without salt, without onions, without ham or bacon, and, as a result, without flavor.

Because it's dark and cold inside, I suggest we have lunch on the terrace, and I busy myself wiping down the chairs and table, pleased that we can at least sit in the sun. She invites Luke to join us, but he declines, and I think I detect a wink in my direction. *Not* your *aunt, you lucky devil!* I think to myself, but I don't say anything, knowing that he knows anyway.

Luke finishes his tasks. Aunt El asks what the damages are and complains about the price, all the while writing him a check and flirting outrageously. Luke picks up Winston and they leave.

I've been there only a half-hour, but I feel a twinge of envy nonetheless as they depart. Aunt El and I sit on the terrace. She asks, "So how's Mike?" and before I can answer, she continues her own train of thought. "I called him, you know. I wanted some advice about the house, but he was too busy to talk with me."

Smart, I think to myself, but again remain silent.

She continues, "He's so self-absorbed, so selfish. All he thinks about is himself; he never has time to help, doesn't care about anyone else—certainly not about me. But then, why should he?"

Another Gemini, I think to myself. *You two are exactly alike. At least you understand each other—and Mike was onto you before I was. After all, he's not a relative, and you're my mother's only remaining sister.* Further, I can't help thinking that her description of Mike is also a perfectly accurate self-description, although she doesn't realize it. I take Mike's side, for a change, and suggest, "How about a little compassion? He isn't feeling all that great, you know, and he's been besieged by all those visitors, which tired him out even more, and he just doesn't have as much energy as he used to. Why do you take it as a personal affront? And besides, what have *you* done for *him* lately?"

I force down the sandwich, aided slightly by a beer, feeling I've earned today's martyr points. And then, again without responding to the direct question, she springs her *pièce de resistance*, "Can you take me down to Sixth and La Brea?"

"Sure," I reply, "when do you want to go? I can take you on Monday sometime."

"Now," she says. These abrupt changes of pace, subject, or thought, which she evidently finds entirely logical, try my patience.

"Moments ago you told me you couldn't leave the house, you wouldn't let me take you out to lunch, and now you want to go to Sixth and La Brea. What for?" I demand.

"To look at more swatches at the fabric store," she replies coolly. "It won't take long. How much time did you say you had?"

I look at my watch. "All right," I tell her. "I'll give you an hour, but I must absolutely have you back here by two-thirty so I can get to my appointment." Already, I'm annoyed at myself for falling into her trap once again.

Then she fixes her hair, puts on lipstick, closes all the windows and doors in the entire house, and we leave. Once we're outside and the place is locked up tighter than Fort Knox, she tells me she must go back to check the gas because she isn't certain she turned off the stove.

I wait. And wait. And wait some more. She finally emerges triumphantly, crowing, "I didn't leave on the gas after all. I only thought I did." When we get into the car, she remarks: "This is a nice car. Is it new?"

"No, Darling," I tell her, "it's the same one you rode in last year."

"I thought it was green," she adds, with a dismissive wave of her hand.

"That was another car," I remind her, "but it wasn't a convertible."

Having lost interest in the car subject, she gives me directions, which are unnecessary since I've been driving in Los Angeles for some thirty years. We arrive at the fabric store, examine yet more swatches, which look exactly like the ones she already has at home. We have yet another discussion about what's practical and what isn't. And then, as we leave, she suggests we stop at two additional stores. I remind her that I'm willing and able to take her shopping on Monday, but she declines because it would interfere with her Monday Afternoon Book Discussion Group.

By now it's two-fifteen on a Friday afternoon, and the traffic is becoming a nightmare. "Just one more stop," she pleads, "so I can pick up my laundry."

Furious, but attempting to suppress it, I head toward the laundry. Traffic is stopped dead, and we can't move. All attempts at conversation have by now ground to a halt, and I *know* that I will be late for my appointment. "I can't imagine what's going on," she admits at last. "Why don't you just take me home?"

Without further ado, I concede. Because I'm late, because she has tried my patience to the nth degree, and because the past two hours have been something between an ordeal and a nightmare, in my haste and dismay, I fail to get out and help her out of the car, which I usually do. She complains about the door, how heavy it is, but refuses my offer to help. Then she manages to exit and slam it shut with considerable energy. (Or is it rage?)

I go off to my appointment. Later that night, while having dinner with my friend Karen— who is also well acquainted with the pixilated complications of Aunt El—she tells me, "Your aunt called this afternoon. She told me you were rude to her, that she couldn't open the car doors because they were too heavy, and you wouldn't even help her out of the car."

Then, cocking her head to the side just enough so I can see the twinkle in her eye, she asks, "Honestly, is this a nice way for you to treat an old lady?"

Hemlock

1990

After a disappointing year attempting to run a serious art gallery in Washington, D.C., I sublet the space and left for a new life. The idea of the gallery was good: five dealers putting together a gallery building in a dicey part of the city, at 406–7th Street, halfway between the National Gallery of Art and the National Portrait Gallery. It was a three-story, existing building, which we reconfigured into one large space on the ground floor, and two spaces on each of the two upper floors.

The building housed one sculpture gallery, one photography space, one devoted to Hispanic art, one owned by an already established local dealer, and my gallery, a combination of old-master and modern prints, drawings, and contemporary paintings. The neighborhood was so rough, which we called "transitional," that one evening per month, when we all changed exhibitions and invited our clients for openings, the street had to be closed off and highly-visible armed guards were uniformed and numerous. Otherwise, our clients would not have attended.

After a year of this, with excellent exhibitions, good reviews, and few sales, it became apparent to me that Washington, unlike Boston or New York, was not a popular or welcoming venue for art collectors. Despite the prominence and cachet of the established museums, monuments, and historic sites, clients rented their art for four years, in case it was time to move on.

Consequently, deciding to take my chances, I moved on to Los Angeles at the age of forty-four. L.A. was one of the few major cities in the country in which I had not already lived. Except for an aging aunt and uncle, both musicians, and one young actor friend attempting a career in film, I knew no one there. I put my furniture, art collection, and inventory into storage and started over, determined to avoid the art business and craft a new life.

The first few months were difficult. However, I found a rundown but centrally-located and potentially cute little cottage in the Hollywood hills. I began to meet people, and I took a job in a well-known and highly respected institute of higher education in Pasadena, where I began as Associate Director of Development and invented a new job and title as Director of Special Events. I also had the opportunity to purchase a splendid Mason & Hamlin grand piano, which considerably enhanced my life and the cottage.

My aunt introduced me to some of her contemporaries, including an eighty-year-old pianist, Felix, who had enjoyed a long and productive career, both concertizing all over the world and hosting a popular radio show in Los Angeles. Semi-retired, he lived in central L.A. with his wife of more than fifty years, Elizabeth, who doted on him like a schoolgirl with a serious crush. Behind their modest, mid-century home, he had constructed a studio, which contained his extensive library of music and two concert grand pianos doing a sixty-nine in the center of the space.

Felix was a whirlwind of energy, small in stature, wiry, committed to music, and knowledgeable, and he loved to play music for four hands and two pianos. I was delighted to meet him, listen to stories of his career, travels, and exploits, then play two-piano music with him every week or two for several hours at a time, following which we would have lunch at an ancient restaurant which he had frequented for his many decades in the business. It was an excellent introduction to Old Los Angeles, and during the next several years, I enjoyed the hospitality and friendship that Felix and Elizabeth proffered so graciously.

After one of our music sessions and following lunch, Felix asked me if I had heard of the Hemlock Society.* My answer was negative, and he asked if he could give me a few pamphlets to read. My curiosity piqued, I took the pamphlets and read them during the next few days.

During our following meeting, Felix asked if I'd read the pamphlets and what sort of response had I felt. I was happy to tell him that the concepts were sound, made perfect sense to me, and that I appreciated the sensibility and mission of the organization.

He seemed unusually excited by this response, and then asked if he might talk with me privately, seriously and confidentially, and of course I responded in the affirmative.

Felix went on to explain that he was an atheist and had always been one and had no use for organized religion of any sort. This was something I already knew because he was never shy about his opinions and beliefs. He went on to explain that he had been diagnosed with a fatal cancer and it was a subject he did not wish to raise or discuss with Elizabeth, because he knew she would be frightened, if not terrified, and he didn't want that to happen. He told me he was frequently in pain, which I had not known, and he did not wish to depart this vale of tears without control of himself. He presented a reasonable argument, to my mind, that he had led a rich and full life and was prepared to exit gracefully, in his own time and manner, and had secured the means to do so. He explained it would be difficult for him to accomplish this on his own, that he could not ask it of Elizabeth, and requested if, when the time came for him to undertake this task, he could trust me to assist him, I would be willing to do so. He quickly added that I should not immediately respond but think about it on my own, decide, and answer in a week or two.

Because he was such an energetic and lively gentleman, I was taken by surprise, but having known him well enough for several years, I felt honored that he was able to trust me so completely with such a serious request. I thought about it for several days, considered how I would feel if I were in his position, and realized that my own response would be identical to his. I would wish the same for myself, if and when the time came, which I conveyed to him at our next meeting. He beamed with pleasure and let me know that he understood what a serious commitment I had made and let me know that he was immensely relieved, reassured he would not have to depart unattended, and extremely grateful.

Just two weeks later, Felix died in his sleep, which I learned from Elizabeth immediately afterward. I was happy that he had passed on quickly, without further suffering, and grateful it was not necessary for me to assist in the process. I was equally grateful that I had accorded him some small measure of reassurance during his final days.

*The Hemlock Society was an American right-to-die and assisted suicide advocacy organization which existed from 1980 to 2003. In 2003, the national organization renamed itself End of Life Choices.

Ask Mr. Brunswick

for Tom Villard
1991

It wasn't my plan to stay here, and Mr. Brunswick didn't expect it either—clearly! However, Tom had to go out of town and asked me to stay in his house to water the yard, take in the mail, forward his calls, and maintain a semblance of life and activity for Mr. Brunswick. It seemed like a nice idea, and it was. Tom is a very considerate fellow. Realities, however, differ enormously from our ideas about them. Just ask Mr. Brunswick.

Tom's house is situated on the side of a hill in the Silverlake section of Los Angeles. A Mediterranean-style villa, it was built in the 1920s. Looking out over the Ivanhoe Reservoir, the property has a splendid garden, a swimming pool, and spectacular views. The interiors are quirky, colorful, amusing, and wonderfully cheerful. From early morning until after sunset, the entire house is filled with light. All in all, it's delightful.

For the past two weeks, I have totally enjoyed the views and the garden. The pool is another matter. It's full of leaves and garden debris; its floor is covered with deep green algae; the pump is ancient and ineffective; and the filter fails to filter. Consequently, it resembles a Vermont pond more than a glamorous Hollywood event. George, the actor-cum-pool man, has been too busy learning how to be an actor-cum-food expediter to take care of the pool. (In case you're wondering, a food expediter makes sure the plates get from the kitchen to the correct waiter.) I presume this is a position which exists only in large restaurants, where the chef has not made the acquaintance of the waiters, but it's not my place to cavil. George has answered my calls, but he hasn't had time to deal with the pool. As a result, it's been getting worse and worse, despite my attempts at daily skimming, balancing, filtering, and chemical additives—to the pool, that is.

To make matters worse, Mr. Brunswick has been unfriendly, disagreeable, and stand-offish. When I first moved to Los Angeles ten or eleven years ago, he was friendly. Whenever I came to visit Tom, he seemed glad to see me, as well as other guests, and he always appreciated a good party because he received a lot of attention. Now he's getting crotchety. Tom tells me it's his age, and I shouldn't take it personally.

When Tom left, he put in a supply of groceries and asked me to make sure Mr. Brunswick is served at least breakfast and dinner on a regular basis. I have complied with the request and faithfully exercised my duties. Mr. Brunswick demands breakfast between 6:30 and 7:00 a.m., and he expects dinner to be served promptly at 5:00 p.m. Twice I was late with dinner, and his displeasure was evident.

Last Thursday I had an afternoon job interview which didn't go well. When I returned to the house, I was blue and hoped for a little sympathy and affection. Mr. Brunswick was waiting for me on the porch. I explained in detail what had occurred at the meeting, picked him up, and put him on my lap.

With complete disdain, he lifted his tail, jumped off my lap, moved slightly, just to the corner of the porch. He lay down in full view, licking himself in a variety of extremely intimate spots, as if to flaunt both his independence and onanistic flexibility. Even more upsetting to me, his attitude seemed arrogant and uncaring, in equal measure.

Suddenly it was too much for me to take, and all the repressed Jewish mother in me came out at once. "You ungrateful little bastard!" I yelled at him. "For weeks I've been serving you breakfast first thing in the morning, warming your plate for dinner, and scraping the ants off your dry, caked, crusty, fucking bowls. I've washed dishes for you, cleaned up after you, shopped for your favorite dishes, put out dry as well as wet food, given you fresh water at least twice a day, and now you won't even give me any sympathy or let me pet you. That's what a pet is for, asshole, to pet! You are a mean, nasty, self-absorbed sonofabitch, and you think you can get away with it just because you're old!

"I'm almost as old as you are, and I'm not walking around with any holier-than-thou attitude. I need a little attention and love once in a while, and you have a certain responsibility, too. You aren't in this relationship alone, you know. Go ahead, stick your tail up in the air and walk away! I don't care! Just don't come pussy-footing around anymore waking me up at six thirty in the morning. It's me, me, me all the time with you. That's it! Meow, meow, meow! I've been taking care of the house, taking care of the pool, and watering the lawn, which is more than you've ever done. You lie around sleeping until it's time to eat; then you want instant service.

"Well, I'm sick of it, you hear? I want and need some recognition and acknowledgment, too! You're not the only one in this house who needs petting, you miserable, selfish old bastard. From now on we'll just *see* who's pussy-whipped around here!

"Go ahead, sit there and lick your balls, or what used to be your balls. I'm not impressed. You can twirl tassels on your tits for all I care!"

When my outburst was finished and my anger had abated, I felt incredibly foolish, but somewhat relieved, in truth. Mr. Brunswick didn't give me any grief, start an argument, or ask for a divorce. It was okay.

Now, six weeks later, I still feed him twice a day, clean his bowl, and give him fresh water. Once in a while, if he's in the mood, he allows me to pet him, but the option is his alone, never mine. Knowledgeable friends tell me I was lucky not to get the job I thought I wanted, and because George, the actor-cum-pool man-cum-food expediter, never did come back to clean and adjust the pool, I was obliged to learn how to do it myself. Consequently it's clean, clear, blue, and perfectly wonderful now: balanced, albeit precariously, as am I, in this relationship and in this life.

Living with someone is not easy these days. Not for anyone—especially if you're a cat! Just ask Mr. Brunswick.

♈

The New Macintosh

1992

With advance money I received as a retainer to do a writing job, a privately commissioned history book, I needed to have the best tools. I talked to a few friends, did some research, and bought the brand-new Apple Macintosh Power Book 145. I was told that it was user-friendly and that a visual person like myself would probably enjoy learning the Macintosh system rather than a PC. Further, the design is compact and the instrument itself is completely portable.

It has been almost a week now since I bought the computer, and every day I've practiced. It does *not* seem friendly to me most of the time, and to tell the truth, sometimes I feel like smashing it or throwing it out the window.

I miss my IBM Selectric typewriter: the weight of it, the solidity, the satisfying mechanical sounds it made, the fact that the paper was visible as one wrote upon it. Yes, I miss all that! I'm told I must persevere; that as I become accustomed to the Macintosh, I will learn to appreciate it, value its flexibility, and possibly even *love* it. For the moment, I haven't been able to successfully complete five chapters of the WordPerfect manual, which is, to my present way of thinking, a vast misnomer. There's nothing "perfect" about it!

One of the things that bothers me is having nothing physical to handle. The screen tells me that certain pictures represent folders, but is a folder a folder if one can't fold it?

That brings up the problem of language. All the words are familiar; each has a specific meaning. But within the context of computer terminology, even though the words are familiar, their meanings have changed. For example, in ordinary parlance, we know what a window is. In computerese, a window is a certain configuration on the screen. But then, so is everything else, so that a folder *looks* like a window, if you know what I mean.

Then we must follow menus. Usually, we don't look at more than two or possibly three menus a day. The thought of more induces indigestion. Whereas in computerese, we have an endless series of menus, each serving an astonishing variety of dishes—a sort of gigantic buffet. And this afternoon, it makes me sick.

My mind doesn't work the way a computer works. It's evident that the machine cannot change; consequently, I'm the one obliged to change. And it's amazing just how much I can *resist* change, even when I think or know it's good for me. I've experienced so many changes during the past, fast ten or twenty years, it is frequently bewildering. I often feel out of control; I don't understand so many things anymore.

Now I'm going to take a break, stop writing, and see if I can successfully save this document. (That's what these electronic dots on the screen are called in computerese: a document.) Pretentious, isn't it?

———— ⟨∞⟩ ————

The time changed from Daylight Savings to Standard, and I awoke an hour earlier than usual, at six o'clock. It was a beautiful, sunny morning in San Diego, prompting me to go for a run in the park. Eucalyptus, juniper, and camphor permeated the morning dampness, and the streets were quiet. Street people were sleeping in the park; some of them were beginning to stir. As I returned to the hotel, a woman engaged me in conversation, something I'm not accustomed to before breakfast.

Her name is Laurie, and she lives in the hotel. Her glasses are smoky, which makes it difficult to see her eyes. She is recently divorced after forty years of marriage. She volunteers for a thrift shop and does laundry for HIV and AIDS patients who are unable to care for themselves. She is willing to take two busses to arrive at a church she likes for Sunday mass. I feel this information is inflicted on me rather than shared and announce my conviction that the foolish old man who sits on the throne in the Vatican (wearing a dress, yet) is guilty of murder, and that he is, in my eyes, criminal. *Yes, criminal!*

Laurie mildly agrees that there is some truth to what I'm screaming, but that the Monsignor in her new church isn't like all the others. At that point, it's clearly time for me to go upstairs for breakfast because if I don't, it'll be too late.

Upstairs, a group of blond people of various generations has gathered. Breakfast is the usual: weak coffee, fake milk, tired fruit, stale muffins, and two varieties of boring breakfast cereal. The blond people discuss the wedding they attended last night and their various plane reservations for later in the day—after they've visited the zoo, had brunch, and paid a necessary social call, all in a rush. To me it sounds like a perfectly horrible way to spend the day, so I flee to my room, work on the computer (rather successfully, it seems), take a shower, and get ready to drive to Black's Beach in La Jolla.

The freeway is uncrowded, my anticipation is great, and the weather is perfect. I find the beach with no trouble, although it's completely unmarked.

The beach is much larger than I expected. In fact, it's vast. Men and women, as well as a few children, are enjoying the beach in various states of dress and undress. Lots of people are completely naked, and volleyball games, frisbee, and frolicking in the surf constitute the major activities of the day—except for cruising, which is Numero Uno. In one volleyball game, some of the players are naked, some wear shorts, several wear shorts and caps. My favorite wears oversized striped blue and white kneepads, a matching blue cap, and nothing else; it's the strongest fashion statement of the day! Hang gliders soar overhead, as well as a phalanx of traditional, airplane-type gliders, and I wonder how there can be such a traffic jam of them, all in one place, while elsewhere along the coast, the skies are clear. I suppose they like looking down on the naked bathers. If I were above the beach in a hang glider, I would too.

I walked almost all the way to the end of the beach, when I spied a particularly attractive young man across the marsh. I made my way over, spread my towel nearby, and settled in. After we had become aware of each other's presence, I spoke to him. It turned out he's Austrian, his English is not too good, and it was necessary to speak slowly. That was not a problem since it gave me more time to admire him. He is fair, slim, with well-developed legs (from skiing, he told me) and he doesn't think he's good-looking, although he's wrong about that. We conversed a bit, I made him nervous, and he went for a walk; then returned. He basked in my attention, all the while pretending not to be interested. In fact, we were both interested and remained so for several hours. By then I was feeling baked from the sun and left, but not until after applying several coats of lotion to his pink Aryan skin. We left it at that, with promises to see each other again some time on the beach.

Returning to the hotel and to the computer, I learn to use the ruler, cut and paste, change margins, and justify right or left, wishing I could justify my own existence.

The next day, I awoke early, still unaccustomed to Standard Time. Another reason I was tired was on account of the new Macintosh. I tried to study the chapter on formatting, but it didn't work. Either my heart wasn't in it, I was too tired, my mind was wandering from the day on the beach, or whatever. In any case, I wasn't getting it, so I decided to go out for dinner.

I jumped in the car and headed up Fifth Avenue, intending to go to University. At the corner before University, where I stopped for a red light, a boy crossing the street caught my eye, and I caught his. I pulled over, and he turned back and got in the car. He was dark-haired, slender, sun-tanned, and handsome, except for missing one of his front teeth, He was wearing only shorts and a t-shirt. He asked what I was doing, and I said I was on my way to dinner. He said he was hungry, too, so I invited him to join me.

I told him I wasn't familiar with the area and asked him to suggest a restaurant. He mentioned a Japanese place two blocks away, so we went there. It was closed, so he suggested we try a Chinese restaurant close by, which was open. We sat down and ordered, agreeing to select a variety of dishes and share them. With Chinese beer we embarked on a lengthy conversation, remarkably comfortable and personal considering that we had just met. He told me he was estranged from his family, that his mother was a thief who'd stolen money from his disabled brother and wrecked their childhood; that his father would have nothing to do with him because of his "unacceptable" lifestyle, given that he lived on the street and hustled for a living. I think the story was entirely true. The boy had considerable poise, good manners, a sufficiency of self-esteem—hard-won, I believe—and more attractive for it.

After dinner we returned to the hotel. He asked me if I had anything to smoke. I said yes and brought out my stash, delicately concealed in a Sherman cigarette box. We smoked a bit in a small pipe. He was impressed by the quality of the smoke, with good reason; it's as good as it gets. He stripped off his clothes and introduced me to his dick by name: "Woody." I shook Woody's hand, as it were, and we moved over to the bed, where we remained for an hour or so.

After a shower, he wanted to leave. He also wanted me to drive him across town, which I declined to do, since I'd already paid him the amount he requested, and I didn't feel like going out again. So, he left alone.

For a few moments I felt like a schmuck, not wanting to drive him home. Then I suddenly realized my stash box was missing. The fucker had stolen my stash! How could he? And after I'd treated him so well! And taken him to dinner! I started to laugh to myself. He'd had me! He did his hustler thing, and he did it perfectly. I mean, they are *obliged* to steal something, aren't they? It's part of the game. I did notice, it's true, but I noticed five minutes too late. And then I was extremely glad I had not driven him across town.

So that's what happened, and it was all the fault of the Macintosh, because I couldn't concentrate on it any longer.

Today I worked on Format with greater success. But I decided to skip over Tables—at least for today. I mean, how often does one have to use tables in a narrative anyway?

———∞∞∞———

The next morning the work went better. That is to say, the job went better. I conducted an interview, which was revealing, informative, helpful, and even amusing. When I returned to the office, the two young women who work there were in full swing. Laura and Marsha are both blonde, attractive, charming, competent, professionally pushy when necessary, and always kind and considerate to me. I made a lot of calls, scheduled several appointments, and then set about to transcribe this morning's interview onto the computer.

As I turned it on, I realized several things were in places on the screen where they didn't belong. A group of folders was hovering about the Trash icon. I had tried to put them in the Trash, but they didn't go in; therefore, I was unable to throw them out.

Then there was the question of the folders, which I'd put in Teach Text. That isn't precisely where I intended them to be, but when I was just beginning, I didn't know where else to put them. And at this point, I didn't know how to get them out of Teach Text and into the Learn folder. I asked Laura if she was familiar with the Macintosh programs, and to my surprise and pleasure, she said yes. For the next hour she helped me put my files where they belonged, transferred folders out of Teach Text into Learn, got rid of the Trash, and provided some useful reassurance with grace and tact.

That spurred me on to greater action, and before I left, I'd transcribed the morning's interview and felt as if I were beginning to accomplish something. It continued to bother me that words like Trash, Teach Text, and Learn, despite their familiarity, have become transformed into a computer lingo which is quite foreign, composed of words reconceived and reconfigured by a group of weird, dysfunctional nerds who have little regard for the English language.

The accomplishment felt good because I hadn't slept well last night and needed a mental diversion. First, I couldn't find the book I wanted, so I bought a novel called *Mr. Benson* by John Preston, which is an intense S&M fantasy.

I was just getting into it when the telephone rang, about eleven o'clock. The hotel clerk told me that George was at the desk, asking for me. For a moment I drew a blank, then suddenly I remembered George was the hustler from Sunday night who'd stolen my stash. I couldn't imagine why he was here, and I couldn't imagine his nerve. I told the clerk to send him up, even though I wasn't feeling very friendly toward him.

He breezed in, hoping I hadn't had dinner yet and that we could perhaps go out. This at eleven o'clock at night! I'd already had dinner at eight o'clock. (This made me feel very bourgeois and didn't improve my mood.) I asked him why he'd stolen my stash. He took umbrage, told me he wasn't a thief, and that I'd *given* him the stash. This, as far as I was concerned, was total fantasy, and I told him so. He replied that it didn't really matter anymore since he'd lost it anyway, changing clothes in the park. He'd put it in his sock, it had fallen out, and when he went back to look for it, he couldn't remember exactly where he'd been and couldn't find it.

Then he told me he'd spent all his money on a motel room the night before, that he hadn't eaten anything all day, and did I have anything to eat? I gave him some cereal, milk, and a banana, but not with a lot of charm. He opined that my lack of charm was due to having drunk too much, which was not true in the first place, and which was not the reason in the second. The real reason was that I felt ripped off and didn't trust him anymore. He picked up on that quickly enough, started to make insulting remarks, and then decided to leave. I encouraged him, and he left, much to my relief.

Then I read two more chapters of "Mr. Benson" and could barely go to sleep, which is why I awoke feeling lousy. But I *did* make some progress on the computer.

Since I last wrote, so much has happened. I spent the past four days doing interviews and transcribing them into the computer. I got stuck a couple of times, and Laura helped me. At least she got me unstuck and put the interviews into the correct folder. The principles, however, aren't yet totally clear, and I think I've written some parts to this story which should appear just above this paragraph, but they don't. Maybe I transferred them to the floppy disk, which I left in the office building for safekeeping.

Last night I worked late, transcribing an interview. When I was finished, I clicked Save, typed in the name for the new document, and felt quite pleased with myself. Afterwards, I couldn't retrieve the document and felt less pleased. I allegedly saved it, so it must be in there somewhere. I hope Laura can help me find it.

My friend Mark called yesterday to tell me that another Los Angeles friend died Wednesday, of a massive heart attack. At least he went quickly! And he was eighty-eight and had enjoyed a rich, full life. But to go two days before his wife's birthday, which is today. How awful for her!

I was planning to go to Los Angeles for a weekend of fun and games, especially given that it's Halloween weekend. That's all changed now. The pretend macabre has given way to genuine macabre.

Meanwhile, I'm packing to leave the hotel. When I return, I'll take Marsha's vacant apartment for a month—another chapter in the San Diego experience. And while I'm in Los Angeles I'll pick up a printer, which will be a new chapter for the computer experience!

As if to complete the full circle of my hotel sojourn, George has arrived once again. My anger has abated. He is tired, hungry, and dirty. He asks if he can take a shower, and I say of course. I give him a drink, some cheese and crackers. We talk for a while, and I ask him if he wants to have something to eat. He replies yes, so we drive up to University and I park the car, suggesting we go to the City Deli. By then he's changed his mind, says he doesn't like the City Deli, that he doesn't want to sit down, and that he'd rather go to Bob's Big Boy. I have a rule about not going to Bob's Big Boy, which is remarkably like my rule about not going to McDonald's. But George, I'm sure, is not interested in my rules, so I give him ten dollars and he gives me a big hug and goes off into the night, while I go to the City Deli and have my solitary soup. Smiling.

My friend Burton came to visit today. Burton is the dean of a major university in Massachusetts, which he refers to as "the F-squared H," which means "the Fucking Filth Hole." Although that's not a particularly attractive introduction to Burton, in fact he's an erudite, intelligent, well-read, sensitive, refined, and scholarly gent. The reason he's here in California is to attend a conference up the coast in Costa Mesa, and since he'd never visited San Diego before, he decided to drive down, test his skill on the freeways, and let me show him the city. Let me add that Burton and I have been friends for more than twenty-five years, and at this point we are the last survivors of what used to be "our" group in Boston in the late sixties and early seventies.

His visit was a good excuse for me to get out of the office and away from the computer for a day, especially because yesterday I spent three hours learning the Dot Matrix printer, with considerable help from Laura, who has proven herself an angel of patience and mercy. The result of these travails was my first printed document: ten pages of this story, first by the fast-print, poor quality technique, then by the best-quality technique to see the difference. Finally by the medium-quality, which is almost as good as the best, but much faster to print. I am not a master printer—far from it, but at least it's a beginning. And to prove it, after Laura left the office, I wrote and printed a letter all on my own.

In any case, I felt I deserved a day off, and furthermore, the weather cooperated perfectly. I awoke at seven, the sun was up and out, and I began the day with a run along the harbor. These runs are always pleasant—especially just in front of the two restaurants at the beginning of the run, where garbage from last night, awaiting pickup, reeks of dead fish. It's a moment of stunning odoriferous intensity, which is somehow always a surprise so early in the morning. After that little jolt, the harbor air seems remarkably fresh and delicious.

I invited Burton for a walk along the harbor, noting various landmarks, pointing out the contrast between the aggressive contemporary high-rises and the older, low-lying, Southern California, Mediterranean architecture, which seems so much more at home in this gentle climate. We walked past the convention center, past the twin, curved towers of the Marriott, then inland, past the Art Deco splendor of the Paladion Shopping Center (the upmarket mall). We wondered at the post-modern pushiness of Horton Plaza (the middle-class mall). I can't help but wonder what "Father" Alonzo Horton, the quintessential, Victorian gentleman entrepreneur and founder of the modern city of San Diego, celebrated for greeting visitors in a frock coat, would think of the rather appalling mall which bears his illustrious name. We looked at the renaissance-style ceilings and opulent lounge of Home Fed Bank, originally built in 1924 to house the multifarious enterprises of John D. Spreckels. We admired the sober elegance of the U.S. Grant Hotel, built at enormous cost by the son of the victorious general. We sauntered past the Downtown YMCA, speculating on the breadth and variety of sexual encounters which must have occurred there during and after the Second World War, when so much of the U.S. Navy was stationed there. We observed a moment of silence, since it would have been unseemly to fall on our knees, given that the sidewalk was torn up for repairs.

For contrast, we got in the car and drove to Coronado Island to have lunch in the enormous, wooden grandeur of the Del Coronado Hotel, still a major tourist attraction and mecca for visitors after more than 105 years. We lunched on a terrace, shaded from the intense heat of the sun by a blue and white striped umbrella, enduring sullen, humorless service from a waiter far too young to enjoy himself so little.

After Coronado, we passed through the Moorish, Portuguese, Spanish baroque opulence of the museums of Balboa Park. We wondered how the inappropriate sixties architecture of the Timken Gallery had ever been allowed, especially for such a lovely group of paintings set within an equally lovely group of historical buildings.

As we strolled, we talked about those other times, those other people, those New England beaches, and our youthful dance with life itself. By the time Burton left to drive back to his conference, I was overcome with sadness. In my mind I have revisited those places we used to go, reviewed the effortless energy we squandered so recklessly, and replayed the songs, the romances, the joys and delights of early manhood. All of these now seem at such remove, given the specter of doom cast over those carefree years by the disease and death of the past decade.

Morning after morning, day after day, night after night, it remains unimaginable: the extent of the loss and the enormity of the AIDS plague. Here it is, a Saturday night, the night to go out, the night to howl, the night to drink, dance, and make merry; the night to forget cares, to get wild, to pick up a stranger who won't be strange by the time he leaves next morning. And somehow, I can't quite bring myself to make the effort. I can't bring myself to get dressed and go out. I can't believe that it will be all fun and games. I can't believe that it's a great idea to get wild and pick up a stranger, much as I crave it. And I also can't believe that I feel this way. Is it age creeping up? Is it fear? Is it hopelessness and despair, or good common sense?

I sit here with the computer, alienated from the world around me, encapsulated in this box of an apartment, redeemed only by hot and cold running water and the electric current, which allows me to play Rachmaninoff trios and Bach suites on a portable Compact Disc player. It's an electronic marvel rather than a warm human, and although I'm grateful to have it, I wish I could trade downtown San Diego for a place with some street life. Genuine street life, with restaurants, cafes, markets, emporiums, and a metropolitan citizenry unafraid to promenade, rather than perform endless, joyless, compulsive shopping in a series of plasticized malls.

Enough of this bullshit! It's time to put on some Levi's and boots and *go out!*

I went out, and it wasn't great. I drove to a bar way out on Kettner Boulevard, where a well-turned-out lesbian told me the bar had changed ownership and was now a women's bar. Tell me about Equal Rights! She said I should go to Wolf's, where "the guys" hang out. I asked her how to get there, and she couldn't tell me, so she asked one of the girls inside. Or at least I thought it was a girl because she was wearing a skirt. I should have known better! It was a guy wearing a skirt, so I asked him if that's how he had to dress to get in. He laughed and said no. He did *not* invite me in; however, he *did* tell me how to get to Wolf's, which is San Diego's leather bar. It was clear across town, but I found it. By then, I wanted a drink—a *real* drink—but they don't have "real drinks," so I had to settle for a beer. I wondered if they had "real men" and wasn't sure. I drank my beer, looked around, felt out of place and left to go home and work on the computer. The Macintosh may not be easy, but at least it doesn't have attitude. And it's a *real* Macintosh.

The next morning was great. I went for an early run along the harbor, then to the office, which was astonishingly quiet, and worked for four hours. Alone, I printed up all the interviews which I'd taped and transcribed during the past two weeks, and everything came out of the printer as it should. I could see that the first transcriptions were awkward. They had spelling faults, spacing disparities, and the usual problems of becoming adjusted to a new machine. The later documents, however, were more coherent, better written, spaced, and edited. I felt I had turned a corner with the computer, so I jumped into the car, went to Black's Beach, and simply enjoyed the afternoon, the naked bodies on the beach, the promenades, the sound of the surf, and the shifting patterns of sun and clouds on the water.

The moon is full tonight, and I have felt as if the moon has been full for the past three days. Sunday night, after the beach, I went out for dinner at an Italian restaurant in the Gaslamp District, took a seat at the bar and spoke with the fellow next to me who turned out to be someone I used to know in Los Angeles ten years ago. He'd shaved off his beard, cut his hair, donned upmarket fashions, lost a lover, found a new one, and is currently in the process of moving to Santa Fe. It was quite a story.

On the way back home, in front of Cartier, a guy cruised me. It was a nice surprise, since no one at the beach had done so, so I cruised him back. He said, "I have only a half-hour." I replied, "In that case, we'd better not waste any time. Come with me!" So he did, and we managed to use the half-hour to our mutual satisfaction. Even better, he took my telephone number, called me back yesterday, and returned for an encore, having scheduled a longer absence from the convention he's attending. He's a doctor from Connecticut, his name is Barry, and his lover of nine years committed suicide without leaving a note. Now *that* is hostile! He's serious; he doesn't drink or smoke because that would interfere with his doctoring. He's incredibly hot, which I think is from having been repressed for too long a time. California is good for him, clearly, and so am I. Furthermore, he needs cheering up, and I can never resist a challenge.

Today is half a holiday. Banks and post offices are closed, but most stores and businesses are open. And I don't think it occurs to many that the entire world should consider a permanent armistice, since the alternatives are so persistently gruesome. Yet Armistice Day gets a half-holiday nod, and tomorrow the wars will resume in full force, while all the merchants who haven't already done so begin gearing up for Holiday Madness. Does this make sense in the grander scheme of things? For me, for mankind, for the planet? I think not.

I have worked on the computer almost non-stop for two days in a row and have developed a huge knot in my right shoulder. At the same time, I have edited and reprinted—with greater skill and speed—all the documents from my first week's efforts. Once again, I wonder: *Does this make sense?*

Two days of research failed to lead to any additional information about the history of printing in early San Diego, and I was feeling discouraged, so I went back to the Historical Society to look at photographs. The keeper of the photograph collection, the man personally responsible for having undertaken the task, was both affable and helpful. With his encouragement and advice, late Thursday afternoon I discovered, one by one, a group of twenty-six photos, dating from 1893 to 1950, representing different stages in the company's history. The subjects of the photos were buildings, interior shots, company picnics, and group portraits. It was an excellent find, and I was encouraged enough to return Friday morning.

Next, his wife, who was equally helpful, brought me out a series of boxes containing several decades of photographs which had been used by the company. The boxes housed thousands of photographs, primarily from the twenties, thirties, and forties, most of which were utilized for various clients' printing needs. It did include, however, several unique and terribly exciting shots of then-new equipment, including presses and enormous cameras. I was elated. So elated, in fact, that I went away for the weekend to Los Angeles, ostensible reasons being both a memorial and a housewarming. Transits in two directions, it seemed, balancing each other perfectly. I put my briefcase and the computer in the trunk of the car and never took them out once during the entire weekend. Now *that* is a successful weekend!

I've been reading all the histories of San Diego available in the libraries, and I feel that in two or three weeks I have learned more about this city than I know about any of the cities where I have lived. That doesn't help when I return to the silence of the rented apartment at night and wish there were someone to dine with, speak with, or even to telephone. Lovely as the climate is, warm as the sun is, there is a blandness here which is inescapable. The streets are mostly deserted, and I am tremendously aware of an absence of life. I wonder, where are all the people who live in this city, who work in the high-rise towers, who live in the endless rows of upscale apartment buildings near the waterfront? What do they do, and where do they do it, and why are so few of them on the streets?

Last night my shoulder ached from too much stress and from too much time on the computer, so I gave it a break, turned it off, and read a book, George Orwell's *Down and Out in Paris and London*, published in 1933. He paints a grim picture, and my dreary apartment looked considerably better to me by the time I'd finished the book.

This morning I went to the Historical Society to work on photographs, but they wouldn't let me in, claiming their regular hours are only Thursday through Saturday, from ten to four. Last week Susan told me I could come in Wednesdays, as well, but today Susan wasn't there, and I was dismissed abruptly.

Much as I have learned about San Diego and its history, I have gleaned almost nothing about the company I've come here to research. Descendants of the founders have promised to come up with old photographs, family files, and company documents, but thus far I've seen precious little, and I'm feeling frustrated for lack of information, for lack of historical facts.

And then there's Tom's birthday party this coming Saturday. Tom has informed all the guests that drag is mandatory. Well, I've never *done* drag, and I'm not *interested* in doing drag, and I don't think I will ever be even remotely attractive in drag. In addition, I'm stuck down here in San Diego, and getting up in drag—if one is to do it properly—is best accomplished with a small group of like-minded friends, and I have no intention of going out shopping for oversized, flamboyant women's clothes and shoes, alone, in an unfamiliar town. I'm annoyed at Tom for insisting that I come in drag, and I'd like to not go to his party. At the same time, I hear a nagging voice in my head reminding me that Tom is not well. This could possibly be his last birthday party, and I am being both a prude and an uncooperative friend. I should do what he wants on his birthday because it is, after all, *his* birthday. For years I've been telling people that on that day, if no other day, we should all *get* precisely what we want and *do* precisely what we want, insofar as possible, for a change. I'm in a quandary. I have nothing to wear!

Last night I called my dear friend Karen to complain. I was thrilled to hear that she feels the same way about this party as I do. In fact, it's even worse for her because, in the first place, she's had enough trouble with men lately. In the second place, she's not keen on finding herself surrounded by a bunch of handsome men in dresses. She admitted that she'd rather they be in pants or out of pants—but NOT in dresses. I admitted that I feel almost the same way I usually feel in a gay bar, which is that it's really not worth it to be gay if this is what one is obliged to endure. Smoke, stale air, weak drinks, and bad music at an unconscionable volume in a room full of men who all want to go home with someone, but clearly not anyone present. And wearing spike heels, to boot: It *is* a social, if not a moral predicament! I admit, I felt a little better when Tom's father told me he was going to come as the Flying Nun—either that or Mother Fucker. (Tom's father weighs more than two hundred pounds, and he's going to be one hell of a nun!)

It was time to leave the office, and Laura said, "Let's go have a cup of coffee. I have to wait until my mother arrives."

I replied, "No, let's get a drink instead."

We went to the pushy Italian restaurant next door, sat at the bar, ordered martinis, and I told her about the telephone ringing at three in the morning with a breather on the line. (No! It was NOT amusing. Not at three in the morning! Had it been eleven at night, now that would have been a different story!) And I told her about the drag party and my quandary. Telling it all made it seem less important. Then her mother arrived, and they went off to the mall to buy Laura her Christmas outfit. Their game is that Laura chooses it, whatever she wants, and later her mother picks it up, wraps it, and puts it under the Christmas tree. On Christmas morning, Laura gets to open it and act surprised.

Well, I survived it. The weekend AND the drag party. I left Friday afternoon at three o'clock, and it took three hours to get to Los Angeles—just what I figured for rush hour. Jeff had the martinis ready, and we were grateful—so grateful that we drank one or two too many, not to mention some aquavit, which had been frozen in a block of ice full of herbs and orchids. By dinner time, none of us was in any shape to go out to dinner, so we ordered pizzas and salad and stayed in.

Saturday morning was a bit rocky, at first, but not impossible, and lots of black coffee helped. My friend Alex and I went over to another friend's house and moved my harpsichord because I thought Alex should have an instrument in the house. We went to a tiny Mexican restaurant and ordered molé. The walls were painted a combination of vermilion and Kelly green, a fake parrot sat on an unused coat rack, and it felt exactly like being in Mexico. The molé was delicious, and afterwards I had indigestion so I know it was genuine. Then I took a nap before going to Tom's for the drag party.

On the way over I wore jeans and a cowboy shirt for some butch reassurance. When I arrived, his parents were already there, and they kibitzed while we put on our makeup. I had already told Tom that I wouldn't do it unless he helped me, which he was only too pleased to do. (Tom has an entire arsenal of bases, varicolored eye shadows, liners, false eyelashes, eyebrow pencils, lipsticks, and powders.) It required more than an hour to do our faces, and afterward we had to get into our "outfits." He had set aside for me white tights, white spike heels, a fouffy, multi-colored skirt (indecently short, with a large pink bow in back), a tight tube top, a brunette wig, and masses of tulle to use as a wrap. I put a pink turban over the wig and completed the ensemble with long white gloves and a hot pink clutch bag, and some of Alex's handmade jewelry—the real thing.

When all was said and done, I looked like a tired old floozy who was trying too hard to stay young. Tom, meanwhile, was enjoying himself thoroughly in a "gown" he'd made himself and characterized as "the Tooth Fairy on acid," which is a fairly accurate description, except that you can't begin to imagine the wig, which was platinum, a beehive, and about three feet tall. So tall that it was impossible for him to get through doors without bending or kneeling.

When we'd finished getting dressed, Tom's father got into his nun's outfit, complete with thick stockings and sensible shoes, and went, finally, as Mother Fucker, while Tom's mother put on a red cardinal's robe, a gold miter, and went as Cardinal Sin. By then, everyone else began to arrive, and all the men were dressed as women and all the women as men. It was very odd and more than a little confusing: all those Amazons and all those little guys, besides which we all had to wear nametags, giving fanciful names to our "new" identities.

The makeup and false eyelashes I found uncomfortable, and the high heels were even worse. I felt foolish rather than glamorous and was unable to get into the spirit of being either a real girl or a real drag queen, as some of the guys could do only too well. Envy, however, did not raise its ugly head. Afterwards I took off the outfit, wiped off the makeup, and put on my jeans and cowboy shirt before going back to Alex's, feeling ultraconservative, since everyone else arrived and departed in his or her outfit, except for one boy whom Tom asked me to help with his makeup since I was now such an expert. The next morning, I still had traces of paint on my face, and my feet hurt from the spike heels. I can't *imagine* how women do it!

The photographs taken at the party confirmed my worst fears. Tom, on the other hand, was delirious with joy. He thought it had been the Best Party He'd Ever Had, and he was thrilled that so many of his friends had gone to so much trouble and gotten so amazingly decked out.

Since then, I've been practically locked in with the Macintosh, trying to finish my book. Last Tuesday, in some despair because it is impossible to find facts and documents for the first fifty years of the company's history, I spoke to the president. I explained the situation and offered him the opportunity to gracefully abandon the project before it goes any further. He read the preface and narrative which I'd produced, looked at the photographs, and asked me to continue, with the understanding that the book will be more a photographic history with illustrative text than vice versa.

Meanwhile, I gave up the apartment I had occupied and moved back to the hotel where I'd stayed previously, since it isn't certain how much longer I'll be obliged to remain in San Diego.

Imagine my surprise when the telephone rang in the hotel room yesterday morning at seven o'clock. It was George, the hustler from the previous month, who'd recognized my car and decided to pay a call. He was wearing a red sweatshirt and cutoff jeans. He was cold, damp, and hungry, having spent the night in the park. He proudly announced that he'd given up crystal meth and that he'd gained weight. He wanted a shower, a joint, a chocolate bar, and thirty dollars in return for a blowjob. He was remarkably unsympathetic to my disinterest, given that I had to dress for an early appointment. I let him take a shower, I gave him tea and a chocolate bar, but I was not inclined to give him thirty dollars or a joint, and I wasn't in the mood for a blowjob.

We had words, then an argument, and although I felt sorry for him, I was not pleased to begin the day with an argument not of my own choosing. I am not responsible for him or where he sleeps or doesn't sleep, and his demands and his intransigence got me so riled up that I told him never to return or to dampen my bathmat again. We almost came to blows, and then he left. When I got downstairs, he was waiting by the car, already repentant, but by then I was in no mood to have anything more to do with him. Afterwards I felt bad all day long, so I decided to tell the computer, since I can't really talk about it at the office. The Macintosh is responsive, yes, and remarkably less judgmental than I am, whether it's about George, hustling, the company, the job, a letter, a story, or me.

This morning the sun was out after several days of cold and rain, so I went for a run in the park before work. I saw George in the distance, wearing the same red sweatshirt and cutoff jeans he was wearing yesterday. I turned and ran in the opposite direction.

No One Must Ever Know

for David Morton
1993

"I want to be famous," he tells me.

And with looks and a body like that, my young friend, I thought, you could be famous in about two seconds! What I said, however, was, "Famous for what?" meaning, for singing? for acting? for writing? for what?

He answers, "So I can be rich."

"But that's a result," I tell him. "It's the result of *doing* something or *being* something."

"I'll get an agent," he goes on, not answering my question, "and the agent will make me even more famous and richer."

Boringly, I implore him once more, "But you have an agent for writing, or for acting, or for *something*. What will you have an agent *for?*"

With two enormous, deep, soulful, sparkling dark-brown eyes that a Rudolph Valentino would envy, he just looks at me uncomprehendingly and changes the subject.

Now if this dialogue had taken place in Hollywood, or even New York, it would not have surprised me. In fact, this dialogue took place in a small village in Southwestern France, in French, and the young man, Philippe, speaks rapidly, forcefully, and remarkably unselfconsciously. His voice is husky, with a sexy, throaty, buzz to it, and his conversation is rapid, sure, and peppered with trendy slang.

I've known him for about three years, having first perceived him around and about the village. I first noticed him for a regal stance; a ramrod-straight carriage; an angular face with remarkable cheekbones, large, deep eyes; and a dark, slender beauty enhanced by a superb, innate sense of movement. Later, I gave rides to him and some of his chums hitchhiking from the village to one or another of the larger cities and towns nearby.

Finally, I got to know him better as the close friend of another youth who came from northern France to live in my house during a summer vacation.

The truth is that I had lusted after Philippe since first seeing him. He didn't look or act like any of the other village boys. He was taller, more stylish, outgoing, and talkative. He was also very full of himself. Two years ago, a group of us went skinny dipping in the river, and I discovered he looked even better naked than dressed in the baggy Levis, loose t-shirts, and mounds of cheap silver jewelry so much in vogue then. I took some photographs at the time, both color and black and white, both clothed and unclothed. Never shy, he was more than pleased with the results of his modeling.

Our friendship has grown slowly. A kind of jet lag exists between us culturally, educationally, socially, and emotionally, as well as a considerable age difference. All those differences make our approaches and distances odd and fascinating, for him as well as for me. We're quite different animals.

Since I first met him, he's been an apprentice to a baker, he's quit school, he's been in and out of the army, and twice already he's been engaged to be married. Subsequent to a knife fight with an Arab buddy in the barracks, during which he was wounded in the knee, he was hospitalized for most of his military service. He was endlessly bathed and tenderly tended by a brigade of military nurses in a hospital near Bordeaux, who were only too pleased to nurse him back to health from a serious blood infection. He emerged with a slight limp, which somehow makes his appearance even sexier. Released from the hospital, his last several months in the military were spent in an office shuffling papers, and his advisors were then requesting that he be awarded a full pension as a wounded war veteran. Philippe had just turned twenty.

Having returned to the village four days ago after an absence of almost a year, I was pleased to see Philippe shortly after arriving. 1 had gone out for an early jog, partly to fight jet lag, partly because if I don't do it early in the day, I don't do it at all. It was also partly because the morning was slightly misty and cool, a comfortable temperature before the heat of the day makes running a chore. Several kilometers out of town, a truck passed, and I perceived Philippe sitting on the deck, in the rear. He noticed me, as well, and we waved. I figured he'd stop by later in the day, but he didn't show up until evening, just before dinner. I was utterly pleased to see him. He gave me a big hug and followed me to the kitchen where I was in the last stages of preparing a meal for Jeannette and Michel; they were getting ready elsewhere in the house. I asked Philippe to join us, but he declined since he'd already dined, and he said he'd come back later for a coffee. He returned, almost on the dot of ten thirty, and we all sat in the living room while he recounted his life and army adventures during the past year. After an hour or so, Michel went home to sleep, and Jeannette, still suffering from jet lag, retired to her room. Philippe and I were alone for the first time in two years.

I asked him if he wanted to go up and see the view from the upstairs terrace. He said no, no view was to be had because it was too cloudy. Then I asked him if he'd like to see the photo- graph I'd made of him and Bruno, framed and hanging in the upstairs bath. He said no, he'd already seen the photo. Then he stood up, as if to go. I didn't really want him to go, and I didn't think he really wanted to go either, so we engaged in small talk for the next ten or twenty minutes. Then I moved around behind him and asked, "Do you remember last year when I gave you a back rub?"

"Of course," he said. "I haven't had that happen since." I then put my hands on his shoulders. He was as tense as a board. I massaged the muscles in his shoulders and asked him if he was always so tense. "Without a doubt," he answered. "That's how muscles are supposed to be." Then I rubbed his shoulders, his shoulder blades, and worked my way down his back, lean and hard beneath a floppy t-shirt. Over the course of ten minutes or so, he relaxed considerably, but not completely.

"Lie down on the floor" I told him.

"On my back?" he asked.

Quickly, although reluctantly, I told him, "No. On your front."

He dropped down on the carpet, and I straddled his back, pulling up his shirt. His back was long and lean, every muscle perfectly outlined, and he was darkly, evenly suntanned from long hours of outdoor work. Nervous from the physical proximity, as well as thrilled by it, I forced myself to remember to breathe. I worked his back and shoulders for a long time; then worked on his neck; gradually added his sides. The pleasure was so intense I could scarcely stand it at certain intervals, and from time to time I held my breath so long I almost passed out. When he was even more relaxed—although far from truly relaxed—I allowed myself to rub his legs, then his thighs, then his butt, which was as firm as a fine piece of sculpted mahogany. My heart pounding, I told him, "Turn over."

His shirt was still pulled up, and I could see every muscle in his chest and stomach and every muscle in his neck, a sight which filled me with admiration, delight, and disbelief. *How can a human being be so firm? How can a body be so tight?* I wondered. *How can muscles remain so taut, even when relaxed?* I massaged his chest, his pectoral muscles, his rib cage. I rubbed his stomach, then his solar plexus and his sides. I lifted his back from below and rubbed his center, then lay him down and did the whole thing once more. His acquiescence was the only consent required and we didn't talk. Gradually, I moved my hands to his lower parts and massaged his upper thighs, his knees and his calves. Finally, I rubbed my hands over his crotch, gently at first, as if by accident, and when he offered no resistance, but reacted with an almost instant erection, I took a final deep breath, unbuttoned his belt, unbuttoned his fly, and took down his pants.

The situation I'd wanted, hoped for, and fantasized for three years was suddenly in my hands. I had him right where I wanted him, and he didn't object. Rather, the contrary. He loved it. I rubbed my hands over his belly, chest, nipples, and neck. I rubbed his balls, thighs, and throbbing cock. I felt every muscle in his hot young body respond wordlessly to my every gesture. I knew the moment had at last arrived, and that I had to take advantage of it. No question entered my mind, I had no choice. This was the moment of truth.

Fully conscious of every instant, fully aware of the risk and the dare I was taking, I leaned over and wrapped my mouth around his cock. I took it in and felt it there, hard cartilage and soft skin, finally where I wanted it, deep in my throat. I moved my lips up and down, slowly and carefully. I felt his cock stiffen and throb. He didn't say a word, and he didn't budge from his position prone on the floor. For a long time, he didn't dare move at all, then he raised his hips. I touched his entire body with my hands, I let my mouth work his cock as it had never been worked. I knew that no woman or no inexperienced boy can suck cock the way I can. I gave him my best, and he knew it. He felt it, because at one point, he leaned up, which caused his belly to tighten even further. He looked me in the eye, took my head with both his hands, and held my head gently but firmly as it moved up and down over his cock. Not long after that, he came in my mouth, quickly, with no warning. It was fantastic. He lay there, not moving except for shooting in my mouth. When he finished coming, his dick softened quickly and still he lay there. For a long time after I swallowed, I lay there as well, his soft cock still in my mouth.

Then abruptly he sat up, saying, "I can't believe it. With a buddy. With a friend. I mean, I can imagine doing this with a chick, but not with a guy." He leaned over, still sitting on the floor, holding his heels, his head on his knees, his pants still down around his ankles.

I took hold of his shoulder and said, "Thanks." He looked at me questioningly, and I repeated: "Thanks, Philippe, that's something I've been wanting to do for a long time."

He went through the "I can't believe I did this—I've never done this with a guy before—I'm not interested in guys—I only have sex with women" routine once more, and once more I reassured him.

"It's okay," I told him. "All men like to have their dicks sucked, even straight men. It doesn't mean you're gay. In fact, it doesn't mean anything except that it feels good." I couldn't help adding, referring to his stay in the hospital due to the knife fight, "And it won't put you in the hospital for weeks or months!" The obvious truth of which brought a smile to his lips, at last.

I felt I had to know and asked: "Is this really the first time you've ever been sucked off by a guy?"

He replied, "Yes, and no one must ever know about this. No one! This will never happen again. *Never!* This is the last time!"

I suggested gently, "Don't make too many rules for yourself. It's only the first time. You should congratulate yourself for trying something you've never tried before. I think you're incredibly brave. In fact, you don't have to congratulate yourself—I'll do it for you!"

Once again he says: "No one must ever know about this. No one! Never!"

"I won't tell," I respond. "Will you?"

He just looks at me, without anger or dismay; more with surprise and wonderment. I continue, "This is our secret. No one will ever know except you and me. We know. You and I both know. That's all that matters, isn't it?"

Then he pulls up his pants and looks me in the eye. I look him back in the eye and ask, "How about a drink?"

"Yes," he answers. "I could use a beer."

"What kind?" I ask.

"Any kind," he replies.

We have a beer together, standing in the kitchen, making small talk, and he prepares to leave.

"I'll stop by tomorrow," he says, in his usual friendly, forthright manner. As he opens the front door, he adds, "Just to say hello. Then on Saturday, I'll introduce you to my fiancée. I want you to meet her, but I won't see her until Saturday. Tomorrow I'll just stop by to say hello." Over his shoulder, as he fades into the darkness of the marketplace, he adds, "But no massages."

Never one to miss an opportunity for the last word, I whisper into the night, "We'll talk about that tomorrow . . ."

$$\Upsilon$$

Off the Record

1993

Off the Record is a shop for used records and compact discs on 5th Avenue, in the San Diego district known as Hillside. A half-hour before the movie next door began, I entered the shop to have a quick look around and discovered six CDs I wanted to buy. I was concerned about their condition because all had been used. Or "pre-owned," as the euphemism now goes. Or perhaps it's only Cadillacs and expensive foreign cars which have been pre-owned. Fords, Chevrolets, and non-new CD's are probably just "used."

In any case, the young man at the counter, with a shaved head and a single dangling silver, assured me that all merchandise was guaranteed. If one of my choices proved to be faulty, I could return it for full credit. That was Thursday night, and because I left town for the weekend early Friday, I was unable to play my used (or pre-owned) CDs until Monday night.

All six of the CDs I chose had musical value and nostalgic value. I bought two Aaron Copland recordings: "Appalachian Spring" with Leonard Bernstein conducting and "Rodeo" and "Billy the Kid" with Leonard Slatkin conducting. The Bernstein recording also included Sam Barber's "Adagio for Strings" and his own "Candide" overture. I also bought a recording by Michael Tilson Thomas, both playing and conducting Gershwin, as well as an album of Bernstein songs from a variety of shows.

It counts for something that I met Aaron Copland on several occasions. It also counts for something that his cook was a friend during a period of our lives which was dramatic, youthful, and, as it seemed to us at the time, momentous.

The time was 1973, and the friend was not yet Copland's cook. He was my neighbor in Provincetown, where I was running a Summer art gallery, and his name was Sophronus Mundy, which was about as perfect a name as I'd ever heard. He lived up to his name, and that summer he became a local celebrity in that his boyfriend, Richard Mayor, committed suicide. We all assumed the suicide was a result of unrequited love for Sophronus, which indeed seemed to be the case. Richard's death was not at all Sophronus' fault, and he certainly was not pleased to be the object of such unfavorable attention. Within a year or so, he went off to become Aaron's cook in upstate New York, and we didn't see much of him after that.

And it counts for something that Leonard Bernstein was a long-time friend as well. For the dozen years I lived in Boston with my partner Eddie Donhowe, from 1966 to 1977, whenever Lenny and various friends and members of his entourage came to Boston, it was my pleasure to entertain them, and our parties for Lenny gained a certain renown, if not infamy, although to my knowledge no one ever committed suicide on account of or a result of them.

The first time we gave a formal dinner for Lenny, after the 1973 Norton Lectures he delivered at Harvard, I handpicked the guests with great care, given that our dining table at the Beacon Hill house seated eleven people, exactly. I remember cooking all day, and Eddie laid the table with special care so that everything would be perfect. Lenny made a grand entrance, late, bringing four extra guests, invited at the last minute, which I had not anticipated. Seeing the table set for a proper dinner, he announced, "I *hate* sit-down dinners. Just give me a plate, and I'll take it upstairs." (The living room in that house was upstairs; the kitchen and dining room were on the ground floor.) There was no choice but to convert the dinner into a buffet, whether I liked it or not.

The second time Lenny arrived for a party, not to be caught unaware, I planned a buffet and invited a larger group of friends. In that instance, Lenny made a point of promptly seating himself at the dining room table, and naturally everyone who could followed suit, leaving the rest of us upstairs with the buffet. That seemed to me perverse on his part, and I decided that sometimes *noblesse* did not necessarily bring *oblige*.

Directly or indirectly, because of my friendship with Lenny, at one of the parties in New York at The Dakota—hosted by Lenny's good friend and neighbor, Mendy Wager—I met a tall, handsome, German-born architect, Manfred Ibel. Manfred, in addition to his roguish good humor, attractive accent, long lean body, unique personal style, and remarkable clothing (which he designed and made himself), also played the flute and had served as muse to Samuel Barber for a lovely flute piece, which ultimately became the slow movement for Sam's piano concerto.

As an architecture student at Yale, Manfred had gotten involved with Sam during a difficult period after his breakup with Gian Carlo Menotti. Although I was not to meet Sam until several years later, Manfred and I were to meet many times over the next twenty years—in New York, Boston, Vermont, Florida, California, and Europe—and we enjoyed a rich and satisfying friendship until his death just two weeks ago.

It also counts for something that a few years later, I was introduced to Sam, with whom I developed a strong friendship, even though Sam was advancing in years and was, in direct proportion to his years, becoming increasingly disillusioned and embittered. Curiously enough, it was not Manfred who introduced us, but Richard Snyder, whom I had met through Michael Tilson Thomas. Michael and Richard had grown up together in Los Angeles, had remained loyal friends since childhood, and it was Richard who introduced me to Sam in 1978.

Having moved there from Boston at the request of Bernstein, who was undergoing a period of personal problems following the death of his wife Felicia, I was relatively new to New York. Beginning in July of 1978, I was asked by Lenny's manager, Harry Kraut, to accompany Lenny to Tanglewood, to New York, to Wolf Trap, back to New York, then to Washington, and back again to New York. Lenny was in a terrible mood almost all the time, most of his staff had quit, and Harry had asked me, as a friend, to help. During those stays in New York it was a relief to spend an occasional evening with Sam, who was mellow in comparison, and he was grateful to have a dinner companion, to have someone to converse with, and someone who would both put with and appreciate his caustic wit and disparaging remarks.

No virtuoso, at the time I was a competent amateur pianist. I played Schubert and Mozart four-hand sonatas with Michael, the Dvorak four-hand pieces with Christoph Eschenbach, and sometimes, Lenny himself would deign to prove he could play louder and faster than I could in a four-hand session which resembled a contest more than a musical event. I liked the *idea* that I was playing four-hand sonatas with Leonard Bernstein, but the reality, in fact, was less enjoyable than the idea of it.

I also loved Sam's piano music but found it difficult to play, and one day I asked, "Sam, why don't you write some piano music for people like me—people who can play, people who love your music, but are not virtuosos?"

His response was typical Barber: "So why don't you learn to play better?"

Sam was a close friend to John Browning, for whom he had written the piano concerto and who gave its first readings. Sam had decided that John and I might be a good combination, and he arranged a dinner for us to meet. John possessed the most beautiful piano I had ever seen, heard or touched—a 1937 Hamburg Steinway, made of a light-colored fruitwood, with a perfect finish, a perfect action, and perfect sound. And Sam was right. It was lust at first sight, and John and I were an item for a few months. The romance was not destined to endure, but it was swell while it lasted, and the friendship with Sam continued nonetheless, despite his snide remarks about my piano playing and most everything else.

In July 1978, I traveled with Lenny to Tanglewood, where we were lodged in Saranak, Koussevitzky's house. My job was to help him quit smoking, to ease the pain of his reaction to Felicia's death, and to help him during the dénouement of his great love for Tommy Cothran. Every morning, I insisted he go for a run, whether in the Berkshires or in Central Park. That was never terribly successful. I also helped him through his traumatic birthday event at Wolf Trap, which he faced with enormous anxiety. He had always been a Whiz Kid, always young and precocious, and he hated turning sixty. It was a painful time.

Through those ups and downs with Sam, Lenny, John, and Mendy (with whom I had embarked on a grandiose, although ill-fated, loft project in lower Manhattan), I always remained friends with Manfred, who was my exact contemporary, having been born one day ahead of me. We shared what I suppose are typical Aries characteristics, although each of us considered himself complete and unique.

Two weeks ago tonight, I spent my last night in the Park Row apartment in San Diego. I was glad to leave, because the complex is too secure, too yuppie, too saccharine, and too inhumane. Gates are everywhere, with special card keys to open them. There are guards, splashing fountains, manicured walkways, tiled courtyards with cutesy names, a heated swimming pool (which is usually deserted), a jacuzzi where, if you dare go in, you must be appropriately attired, and prominent signs which advise you not to go in if you are pregnant, intoxicated, under the influence of drugs or narcotics, or alone. That eliminates almost everyone in the complex.

That day, I worked late and returned about seven thirty. Because the apartment was basically unfurnished, it was depressing. And even if it had been furnished, it would still have been depressing because it's small, dark and situated at street level, with people living above. Only one thing is worse than people living above you: the *noises* emanating from people above.

Feeling blue, I couldn't stay inside, so I walked up to Horton Plaza, hoping to buy cartridges for my Parker pen. It seemed a simple task. *Not.* I visited four stores in a row, including a Hallmark store and a major drugstore. Miles and miles of merchandise sat on their shelves but no Parker pen cartridges. As a last resort, I stopped at the Mark Cross store in the upmarket mall across the street, where two very snooty clerks were only too delighted to inform me that they carry *only* Mark Cross merchandise. Even more distressing than the fact I couldn't get what I wanted was the series of loudspeakers in sequence screaming "Jingle Bells" through the mall, so there was no escape possible.

"Jingle Bells" is not now a great song, was never a great song, but it can be endured, on occasion, for a moment or two, in the right place, in the right mood. But broadcasted at top volume, in a public mall, in November, in San Diego, California—where there never is and never will be any snow, let alone any sleighs— and where horses are as long gone as the Pony Express . . . this seems to me to be stupid beyond belief. And it is!

Depressed by the mall, by the seemingly impossible task of finding a couple of ink cartridges, and the relentless noise pollution under the guise of holiday music, I returned to the apartment. It was quiet, except for the tiresome splashing of the quaintly-tiled, pseudo-Spanish fountain outside, so I put on some music, made a drink, and hoped the telephone would ring.

Sure enough, it did. It was Tom Singer calling from New York to tell me that Manfred had died. Then he told me details of the preceding weekend: who was present there in Key West, what they all did, the music Tom played, and how Manfred had orchestrated his own farewell events. Then Tom described the cremation, the memorial planned for the Winter Solstice, and the White Party to follow, given that Manfred was famous for his annual White Parties.

I can't say the news was totally unexpected, but on the other hand, it's never good to learn that yet another friend has left this vale of tears involuntarily. Especially since he's exactly my age, plus one day. Or was. And by the time Tom had finished, and I had hung up the phone, I wondered why it was that I'd wanted it to ring. It's one of those half-assed, incomplete wishes. And now I can't stop thinking about Manfred—his multiple talents, his enormous creativity, his iconoclastic way of life, his ferocious independence, and his love of music and musicians. I would miss his sensible, matter-of-fact European attitudes towards life and love, his vitality, his fondness for Asian gardens, his tender appreciation of his friends, and his austere esthetic sensibility. I loved the wondrous sense of costume he enjoyed, his amazing original clothing designs, those great jeans he invented and could never get manufactured, and his lilting use of English with just a trace of the original German softening the rough edges.

Further, I'm feeling guilty, although we were in frequent contact. I could have been a better friend. I could have made more of an effort to pay a last visit. I could have written more and telephoned more. And yet, we did talk on the phone, and we exchanged letters. I knew how depressed he was by this debilitating series of maladies. He told me over and over how he couldn't believe it was happening to him. He hated to feel his energy, diminish, his vitality depart. He hated feeling sick, depressed, and dependent. Who could blame him? Who wants to feel sick, depressed and dependent? Certainly not an Aries who had been supremely physical all his life. Certainly not a man who lived on brown rice and vegetables. Certainly not someone who bathed himself in minerals and douched out the poisons of New York City long before anyone else had thought of it, using a series of devices he invented himself and had installed in that brilliant, unusual, all-white apartment on Fifth Avenue; the one with the pyramid in the bedroom, the bathtub on a pedestal, and the swing in the hallway.

Manfred's death two weeks ago has reminded me painfully, once again, of my own mortality. Now Sam is gone, Lenny is gone, and Aaron is gone. So is Sophronus, and so are scores of friends, lovers, parents, relatives, and acquaintances. John is still above the ground, but we no long speak or communicate.

Once again, I'm living in California or in France, and that dazzling, brilliant, melancholy, sophisticated, glamorous and remarkable although unsatisfying New York life we all shared ten or twenty years ago is forever finished. That era is past and gone, except in the interstices of our individual, as well as collective, memories and hearts, and in the complicated intertwining of our lives as they now play out, on and off the record, in the rainbow-hued laser grooves of our own gay nineties.

♈

Hollywood House Sitter
1993

Albert, my friend who teaches Ancient History at the university, asked me to house sit for a shoot this afternoon because his lover, Ronnie, is out of town on a business trip, and Albert must teach or attend a seminar or something like that. A good part of his life is lived, still, in previous centuries. In the present century, however, they live in a beautiful, contemporary house in the Hollywood Hills, which features a sculptural swimming pool enhanced by a waterfall, hot tub, and private terrace handsomely appointed, with over-scaled ancient urns, all of which is enclosed by ebullient, semi-tropical hillside gardens.

The property is frequently rented by top photographers, still as well as motion picture, and I hoped that today's shoot would turn out to be with Herb Ritts or Bruce Weber and a gaggle of hunky men – but no such luck. It's for *Penthouse* magazine.

I'm sitting quietly in the kitchen, where a caterer is busy preparing lunch. Outside on the terrace, fifteen guys are wielding reflectors; positioning lights, cameras, microphones, and speakers; and fussing with an astonishing variety of equipment. The crew is comprised of two guards in uniform, wardrobe people, makeup artists, and about a dozen voluptuous young women unabashedly exhibiting vast quantities of tits and ass, with more than a hint of pussy. Is this all erotic and intimate? No.

To keep occupied, because these things can go on for hours and hours, I bring along my laptop and set to writing. One of the models notices me working with my portable computer and comes over with questions. She has the grace to put on a t-shirt, make small talk, and proclaim interest. Because she's cute, because I've never been that close before to one of "those" girls, and because it's fun, I invite her to sit down. I show her how to use the laptop, and I let her go through Apple basics.

She catches on quickly, and she's thrilled with the computer. I learn that her name is Shauna and she's writing a book.

Meanwhile, just outside, two guys with buckets are sloshing down the stairway under the waterfall, and a leggy blonde (Shauna tells me her name is Tammy) wearing a low-cut black thing not as large as a bathing suit, and *extremely* high spiked black patent leather pumps, is getting ready to do her striptease, beginning at the top of the stairs and working her way down to a bed at the bottom of the staircase. The music starts, and she begins to undulate. As part of the routine, she turns slowly, meaningfully, all the while looking over her shoulder towards the camera . . . and surprise! There's no backside to her costume.

While Shauna is doing Basics, I can't help but look out the window to watch what's going on. Tammy, who has a Brigitte Bardot type of pouty mouth, has just taken off all her clothes. It amuses me enormously to think of the curious irony that Ancient History has made it possible for Playmates and Pets to get naked in Hollywood, perform strip routines on an architecturally significant staircase, cavort in gently lascivious glee for the camera, and leave wet spots all over the terrace.

It's time for a break...

———⚬⚬⚬———

The first session wraps and the caterer serves food upstairs on the terrace. Every activity stops for the lunchbreak, and the star of the moment is the food. Tammy and Shauna ask if they may join me in the kitchen, and I reply, "Of course." Everyone else remains outside.

Then, over tostadas and chips, some serious Girl Talk begins. Shauna isn't very hungry because someone spiked her drink at the bar last night. She thought, at first, she'd drunk too much, but then realized that the effects of the drink were due to something other than alcohol, and this morning she didn't feel well. She has no idea who spiked her drink or why, but it annoys her.

She continues to tell me about her writing – a Jackie-Collins-type book, she explains, about—guess what? —her boyfriends.

Twice in her young life she's fallen in love with a twin, had a difficult relationship with him, and subsequently gone out with the identical twin brother. Then, in both cases, it was clear to the second twin that she was more interested in the first one, so she returned to the original sweetheart. The very first one, the one she still loves, subsequently got a girl pregnant and married her, but he and Shauna continue to see each other behind the wife's back.

There. I've written her book in three sentences.

Ronnie telephones from Lake Arrowhead, where his company retreat is being held. He allows there's just a little too much peach in the hotel room. I allow the same is true here. Then I describe how Shauna and Tammy dished the bad boob jobs on the two girls who did their routines after lunch. Actually the first girl's boob job wasn't technically bad, because she isn't out of proportion. Standing still, in fact, she's stunning, but when she dances, her boobs don't move, which is peculiar. The second girl is so top heavy as to appear off balance, and her boobs are not only bovine, but completely motionless when she dances, as if they're made of wood. The effect is unnerving, and I wonder how it will appear on film.

Tammy and Shauna, finished filming for the day, decide abruptly to go shopping at the Beverly Center. Departing, Shauna tells me she's up for "Pet of the Month" and she might win if enough people telephone the magazine and vote for her. She adds that her "dirty girl" name is Stevie, so I should call in my vote for Stevie rather than for Shauna.

Now it's getting late, the crew repositions lights and reflectors, and the director asks me to turn on the pool lights and the bubbles in the sauna for some night shots. I oblige, of course. That's what a Hollywood house sitter does, isn't it?

Mendocino Dan

1994

Dan Dearinger
C/O General Delivery
Mendocino, California

The letter was returned to me, marked "unclaimed." Inside was a brief note and two photographs of a handsome lad with high cheekbones, sitting on a rock overlooking the Mendocino shoreline. The note I had sent him read, "Dear Dan, It was a pleasure to meet you and hang out on the beach for a couple of hours. I liked hearing your story and enjoyed speaking with you, except for the Jesus and Bible part, which doesn't appeal to me personally. If you ever find yourself coming to San Francisco, give me a call." I added my phone number, which he never used.

I had been invited to Mendocino for a job interview. It was a warm, late summer day. I drove up Highway 101 through the wine country of Sonoma County, then through the incredible heat of the Alexander Valley, followed by the sparkling light and dark shadows of an enormous redwood forest adjacent to the coast. Because it was so warm, I wore jeans and a t-shirt, kept the top down on the car, and put a change of clothes for the job interview in the trunk. Arriving in the town of Mendocino, I was a few minutes early, so I drove through the town, took a walk down the main street, and eventually stopped to change clothes in a parking lot overlooking the sea. I put on clean chinos, a white shirt, and as I turned the rear-view mirror of the car to tie my tie, the entire mirror assembly fell. Completely off the windshield. So, hoping the tie was all right, I went straight to the interview, which was a few miles out of town, not having time to attend to the mirror. It was strange driving with the rear-view mirror hanging there, slapping against the windshield, but there was nothing to do about it at that moment.

The interview was satisfactory but pointless. I knew that I didn't really want the job, and I knew that they didn't really want me. But we all did what was required, and an hour later I left, slightly annoyed they hadn't invited me to stay for dinner, at least. Driving back to town, I stopped at a gas station to ask if they could fix the mirror. It was five o'clock in the afternoon on a Friday. They didn't have the equipment necessary to do the job, so they suggested I go around the corner and ask Butch at the auto body shop if he could do it. I drove around the corner, where a remarkably fit young man of about eighteen was working on a car. He wasn't Butch, he told me, but the older young man inside the shop came out, looked at the mirror and said that he thought he could fix it. But he said that it would take him an hour or so because it required that much time for the glue to set properly.

Grateful that he was willing to do the job, considering the time of day, I offered to get some beer, a suggestion enthusiastically welcomed. I left the car and the keys, walked to the center of town, found a liquor store and bought a six-pack, figuring that we'd have two beers each: two for the eighteen-year-old who wasn't Butch, two for the real Butch, and two for me.

As I walked back to the body shop, I stopped at the gas station to use the restroom. I opened the door, which was unlocked, to find a half-naked young man washing up at the sink. His dark brown hair was completely wet, and trickles of water were running down his torso, which was beautifully suntanned, elegantly formed, and finely muscled. It was a vision worthy of the finest Italian painter, and I could scarcely believe my good luck.

He looked up, smiled, and said: "You go ahead, I'll wait outside."

I answered, with astonishingly unrehearsed alacrity, "No, don't let me interrupt you. Please continue and I'll just take a leak."

"Okay," he replied, "as long as it doesn't bother you." It did, in fact, bother me, but only in the most pleasurable manner. I asked him why he was washing in the gas station, and he told me he'd just finished working all day as a laborer on the renovation of the church across the way. Watching him bathe in the sink was an intensely intimate, extremely erotic fantasy for me, and I was as surprised by his friendliness and volubility as I was aroused by the possibility of what might subsequently happen. We spoke for a few minutes, and I told him I was taking some beer down to the auto body shop and that he was welcomed to have some if he wanted. We exchanged names, he put on his shirt over his still-wet body and followed along like a puppy.

The eighteen-year-old, who wasn't Butch, was driving off as we approached, and Butch told us that the boy's workday was over, and he was going home. I introduced Dan and Butch, and Butch said that the repair was almost complete. We had beers together while the last coat of epoxy was drying, then Butch sent us off into the sunset, Dan and me.

I suggested we watch the sunset from the beach, and Dan agreed it was a good idea. We drove out to the coast, took our remaining beers, and sat on the rocks. Dan told me about his life, how he'd been a rock musician, quite successfully, how he'd made lots of money, married his high-school sweetheart, and then got hooked on cocaine. He'd lost everything: his job, his career, his house, and his bride. Now he was at rock-bottom and, thanks to AA and Jesus, was putting his life together and starting over. Boldly, I asked him to take off his shirt, so I could photograph him as I'd first seen him, but he wouldn't do it. I then took a couple of photographs of him sitting on the rocks by the sea, and he mentioned that no one had taken his photograph in a long, long time. I told him if he wanted to give me his last name and address, I would send him copies of the photographs. He told me his last name was Dearinger and I could write to him c/o General Delivery.

The sunset waned, I drove Dan back to Mendocino and headed down the coast for San Francisco, hoping I might see him again. The note was returned, and "Dear Dan" never received the photographs.

♈

While Malibu Burned

1994

The November day dawned bright and clear. By nine o'clock, the temperature was already above eighty degrees, a perfect Southern California morning. With no appointments, no lunch date, and nothing else planned, I spontaneously decided to go to the beach. At first the thought of Santa Monica appealed, but because I imagined the beach there to be crowded, I decided instead to go to Point Dumé. (Some pronounce it "Doom," others prefer "Doo-may.") Situated further north up the coast, the shore is less accessible, more beautiful, and few people are willing to take the trouble to get there because parking is at some distance from the beach; after the initial walk, it becomes necessary to descend a steep path and traverse a considerable stretch of rocks.

Arriving at Dumé Drive, it was already ten o'clock, and by the time I parked the car and walked a half-mile to the beach access point, it was almost ten-thirty. To my surprise, I saw a fellow leaving. He pointed behind me and said, "See the fire?"

I replied, "No," and turned around to look. Behind me was a large column of smoke, still far south. "It started in Topanga Canyon," the fellow said, "which means that with Santa Ana winds behind, it'll head towards the beach soon, then Pacific Coast Highway will be closed. So I'm getting out of here. I don't want to be stuck."

Since it had taken me more than an hour to reach Malibu, I wasn't in the mood to turn around and leave instantly, so I followed the path to the beach, descending the long stairway to sea level. Smoke began to drift out over the ocean from the fire, but it was not sufficient to deter me. The tide was high, the sun was bright, and I picked my way across the rocks to the sandy part of the beach.

Two bare-breasted women sunning on the dunes had noticed the plumes of smoke and asked me what was happening. I told them it appeared to be a fire in Topanga Canyon. One of them calmly said, "Oh shit." Without further ado they packed up and left. I continued down the beach and staked my claim to a nice, flat piece of dry sand above the high-tide line.

The smoke became thicker, forming a dense cloud over the sea, obscuring the sun in such a manner that it appeared to be sunset, even though it wasn't yet noon. A curious yellow haze colored the sky, and the foam on the tide appeared golden rather than white. Gradually the sea began to change color, and the blues became purples and greens. The seascapes became ever more surreal, and the light continued to reflect and refract at strange angles. Although eerie, the views were strangely beautiful, and for hours the play of light over the sea changed and altered, a little at a time, creating magical, hallucinogenic-type effects. For once I had neglected to bring my camera. Although I wanted to make photographs, it was probably just as well I couldn't because a great deal of the beauty derived from subtle changes and shifts in smoke, water, sun, and light combinations, which would have been almost impossible to capture on film.

Few people had come to the beach, and those who did figured that for once the police would be engaged elsewhere, given the fire, evacuation procedures, and traffic problems. So all those bold enough to remain on the beach stripped naked to lie on the beach or run into the water. It felt like taking part in a painting by Hieronymus Bosch, given the odd luminescence of the atmosphere, the naked bodies, and the infernal, peculiar colors of the sea.

My eyes began to burn from the smoke in the air, but I was unable to ignore a compelling intensity of the moment which made it impossible to leave. Several times I walked to the point at the southernmost end of the beach to get a better view of the fire, and within an hour, I could see the flames attacking Malibu. The clouds of smoke thickened, grew larger and denser. From time to time the sun became completely obscured by thick smoke, and the wind would shift, creating patches of blue within the yellow-gray skies.

A man with four Rottweiler dogs approached, walking down the beach, and we talked briefly about how strange and beautiful the day appeared, despite the devastation just a few miles away. The dogs, surprisingly friendly and playful, were oblivious to the smoke. A couple of self-conscious hikers with backpacks passed by, while two handsome, naked boys played in the surf. A solitary man lay in the sun quietly reading his book. I shared a sandwich with some seagulls, and a flock of sandpipers ran along the water's edge, picking at invisible snacks.

The final time I walked to the point, standing just below the cliffs, I perceived a naked man with long blond hair, intense blue eyes, sporting an erection. Poised against the rocks, smoke and haze above his head, his body clothed only in a curious golden glow, he was tempting. Irresistible, in fact. I approached, we spoke briefly and had sex somewhat distractedly, on the sand, in the smoky, discolored open air, on the edge of the purple sea, while Malibu burned.

About four o'clock, when the tide receded, I departed. The once-familiar walk along the beach was completely altered by smoke creating varied hues of gray. The sea turned a rich burgundy color, and faded, streaked rays of sun occasionally pierced the overcast. The car, vulnerable with its top down, was parked under a tree which had dropped and scattered seeds and leaves into the open vehicle. I brushed off ashes and debris and drove back to Los Angeles along Kanan Dumé Road. The freeway entrance was congested, but otherwise the drive back to town was clear.

I had no idea how bad the fire had been until I turned on the news upon reaching Alec's house in El Sereno where I was staying. I didn't know how many homes had been burned, or the extent of the disaster which had visited Malibu while I spent the day on the beach at Point Dumé. It all seemed so unreal. But then "reality" is such a relative concept, depending, as it does, so completely on one's point of view.

The next day I learned that a friend of mine, an accomplished writer and stalwart gentleman of more than seventy years, lost in the fire not only his magnificent Malibu house, but his art collection, library, grand piano, clothing, personal effects—in fact, everything he possessed.

The following day, he announced he would rebuild on the exact same location.

Nate's Curious Legacy
(From an Era of Elegance)
1994

Having some errands to run in downtown San Francisco, I decided to walk through Union Square. On the sidewalk directly across from the St. Francis Hotel, a Peruvian band was playing. Overhead the sun was shining brightly on a beautiful day. In immediate proximity to the band, performing in painfully amplified competition, was a would-be chanteuse dramatically attired in black, skin-tight Lycra pants, jungle red spike heels, and a startlingly inappropriate gold and silver lamé evening jacket, which glittered in the sunlight. She was crooning off-key into the microphone of a portable music system, creating a cacophony of noise pollution which sullied the otherwise pristine brilliance and lazy, noontime atmosphere of the Square. All this seemed particularly unlikely to be taking place in full view of the St. Francis Hotel, which was both disfigured with scaffolding and emblazoned with a banner proclaiming its "return to an era of elegance." I wondered if the forthcoming "era of elegance" would prove to be yet another era of hypocrisy, denial, and dissimulation.

I fondly remember the previous "era of elegance," as well as the hypocrisy, denial, and dissimulation which was the curious legacy of my friend Nate—and perhaps of many of his generation. Frankly, I believed it would require far more than a banner on a hotel to usher in a new era of elegance; in addition, as far as I was concerned, a ban on noise pollution would be one of its essential components.

That day, however, sitting then in Union Square, I recalled my first visits to the St. Francis with Nate some thirty-five years previously, which were, in truth, surpassingly elegant. Or so they seemed.

Whenever I arrived for a visit in San Francisco, I would call Nate, and we would get together for drinks and dinner to catch up, learn the latest, reminisce about old times, and enjoy each other's company. This time, when I telephoned Nate's apartment, an unfamiliar female voice answered. I identified myself and asked to speak with Nate. She hesitated with, "Just a minute, please." Then another woman picked up the phone, somewhat embarrassed, explaining that she was a cousin, that Nate had died three days previously, and that they were in the process of removing his personal effects, furniture, and clothing from the building. At a loss what to do or say, because I didn't know her and she didn't know me, I muttered a quiet, "I'm sorry. Thank you." And I hung up.

Having known Nate for more than thirty-five years, I realized in a flash that I didn't know his cousin or his daughter's married name, that I had never been introduced to either his son or his daughter, even though I'd been hearing about them for decades. They never knew me at all; they probably didn't even know of my existence. If I hadn't chanced to call at that moment, specifically, none of his family would have had any means to notify me of his death.

Both Nate's son and daughter lived in Hawaii, but that wasn't the real reason we remained unacquainted. The real reason was that, since his divorce some forty years ago, Nate had lived as a closeted gay man. During that entire period he deliberately refrained from discussing his private life or introducing any of his male friends to members of his family.

At this point, to think of the situation with any semblance of charity, I am obliged to tell myself a generation gap is involved; that men of Nate's generation, class, and position did not go public with private matters, and most of his gay colleagues and peers led equally closeted lives.

That thought, however, was small solace. I felt cheated. I was unable to send a letter of regret or condolences, unable to give or to receive sympathy, and unable to speak of Nate or his death with anyone else who knew him. I didn't know if there would be a memorial service or not, and even if there was one, it was unlikely I would be invited. That put me in a peculiar situation, and although it may have been all right for Nate, since he Got Out, I was still here dealing with conflicting thoughts and emotions about the situation. I did not feel that all was right or as it should be.

In the summer of 1959, when I was twenty-two, I went to Seattle to work towards an advanced degree at the University of Washington, while serving simultaneously as a teaching assistant. I rented a houseboat (atmospheric and inexpensive) moored at a rickety dock on the shore of Lake Union, bought an ancient, abused, underpowered, and supremely stylish Hillman-Minx convertible, and worked at odd jobs to supplement the tiny stipend then given to teaching assistants. One of my jobs consisted of playing background music on the piano at the behest of the university catering service for occasional conventions, dinners, or cocktail parties—a lucrative, although erratic, generally pleasant and undemanding occupation.

At one such event, playing for a convention cocktail party, I became aware of a tall, well-dressed, suntanned, silver-haired gent who several times requested classical pieces rather than Broadway tunes or ballads. With an easy conversational affability, he told me his name was Nate and mentioned he had come to the convention from Hawaii where he lived and did business. Nate paid attention both to the music and to me, which I found unusual, and he bought me more drinks than I was accustomed to having while working. By the time the party was finished, so was my ability to drive. Nate drove me back to the houseboat in my Hillman-Minx. Solicitous and kind, he put me—untouched, as best as I could recall—to bed, leaving my car keys with a note to call him the next day.

The following morning upon awakening, I felt stupid and embarrassed, but not too embarrassed to call him, once I saw the note. I learned that he had taken a taxi back to his hotel. Nate found the incident quite amusing and invited me to dinner. In turn, I found him intelligent, well-educated, sophisticated, and sexy. Further, I was flattered by his attentions, never having previously been admired or courted by an "older" man.

Nate was forty at the time, a former colonel in the army, divorced with two children, a successful businessman, and interested, clearly, in me. I didn't exactly fall in love with him, but I liked him, I respected him, I admired his manner and his success, I enjoyed his company, and I took to his silver tongue and suave refinement like a duck to water. We spent a couple of evenings and nights together, following which he returned to Hawaii and I to my university pursuits.

A few months later Nate called to let me know he'd be in San Francisco during the holidays. Having planned to visit family in the Sacramento Valley, I was delighted to accept his invitation to spend a weekend with him at the St. Francis Hotel. He invited me to dine with him at Bardelli's, his favorite restaurant. We visited a few clubs, attended the symphony and thoroughly enjoyed the elegance and privacy of the St. Francis. During that weekend, Nate arranged with the hotel for my first professional massage, an amazing experience during which the masseur confided that he didn't have many young people from the St. Francis as subjects—or were they "objects"?—and his appreciation, in the form of a blowjob to cap off the massage, was unexpected, unsolicited, unreturned, and completely thrilling. Nate's smile, it seemed to me at the time, was surprisingly blasé when I described to him in glowing detail what had occurred.

A few years later Nate moved permanently to San Francisco, taking a comfortable, conservatively elegant apartment, situated at the very top of Nob Hill, which boasted a splendid view and tasteful, English-Country-Gentleman decor. During the next twenty-five years, he lived in stylish retirement, attending opera and symphony concerts, playing bridge with fashionable ladies, and circumnavigating the globe each year on a luxury cruise ship with the same three friends. He told me the purpose of the cruise was primarily to play bridge, and I was horrified to learn that he and his group almost never left the ship because to do so interfered with their game.

It wasn't a life I could imagine living, and in a way, I felt sorry for Nate. By then, I had come out completely and was living an openly gay life in Boston, with my then-lover Edward. After some years I realized that Nate had become, in some strange way, at least from my overtly gay and comparatively liberated opinion, only half-alive. His sexuality was almost completely repressed, he had no openly gay friends, and his San Francisco social life was as rigid as his gay life was closeted. I was one of his few confidants, and, it has occurred to me since his demise, perhaps even more than that; perhaps I was his Guilty Secret. The choice, however, was his, and I felt I had neither the right nor the reason to criticize him or his lifestyle, especially because he was, in my presence at least, as open, well-adjusted, and generous of spirit as he was hospitable, cultivated, and affectionate. His life—and what appeared from the outside to be a graceful and elegant situation he'd created—was, from my point of view, unsatisfying and unfulfilling.

After completing graduate school, I lived for two years abroad and most of the next twenty years on the East Coast; consequently, my meetings with Nate were infrequent, but always meaningful. We corresponded occasionally, spoke on the telephone from time to time, and if I were in San Francisco or Nate came East, we always met. Our meetings were always pleasurable events, and he was a good friend, a fine conversationalist, a connoisseur of music, and a gentleman of the old school whose company, refinement, sophistication, and good nature I valued.

He was also the sort of man I always wished my father had been, and although our relationship was anything but filial, the generational gap allowed for occasional disparity as well as a great and unusual affection. I admired him enormously, and the feeling was mutual. Nate loved to tell war stories: stories about how it had been for him and his buddies during the Second World War. Adventures in barracks, on boats, planes, and trains were tales he recounted with relish and delight; never with a sense of anger for the inequities of the system that ruined so many military people's careers and lives. And after the War, after his marriage and divorce, he told tales of meeting boys and men in bars and bathhouses. Nate relished the descriptive anecdote and was a master of the form.

Many of his stories I can no longer recall, but this particular one, I couldn't forget. Nate had gone to a bathhouse and noticed an attractive boy of eighteen or twenty who appeared shy and ill at ease. Taking the conversational initiative with his usual tact, Nate subsequently invited the boy to his room. (I can remember perfectly how I felt myself when Nate first turned on his charm, and I could empathize with both Nate and the boy as I listened to the yarn.) The story included lengthy descriptions of the boy's great beauty as well as Nate's appreciation of the details.

According to the story, after the initial moves had been choreographed and a sense of trust was established, at one point the boy said to Nate, with surprising directness, "I want you to fuck me."

Nate complied, as the role required, and as their lovemaking became more heated, Nate was first startled and then dismayed to hear the boy saying, "Yeah, Daddy. That's it, Daddy! Fuck me! Fuck me hard, Daddy, fuck me!" Nate overcame his dismay to find himself increasingly excited by the boy's exhortations. At the moment of climax, simultaneous with orgasm, the boy burst into tears and began to weep uncontrollably. Startled again, this time by the unexpected emotional outburst in what had begun as a simple sexual encounter, Nate held the boy quietly, in what I'm sure was an avuncular, consoling embrace, and when both had regained their composure, the boy departed. Nate refrained from questioning him at the time, and they never saw each other again.

Did the boy have a real-life affair with his father? Was he a willing participant? Did Nate in fact remind the boy of his father? Was Nate caught up in a fantasy of his own design or was he simply an agent employed by fate to realize the boy's erotic fantasy? Certainly, all that was possible. The details of the boy's story are unknown; therefore, that event, as far as I'm concerned, remains both mysterious and anecdotal.

Now Nate is gone, and I, having refrained from criticism when he was here, never having asked to be introduced to his family or friends, have been forced to realize that I, too, dwelt unwittingly in the closet he designed and constructed, presumably for himself. It was my own fault for not forcing the issue, and now, after more than thirty years of our shared friendship, I'm left with silence, no common friends or family, no one to whom I could send condolences and, except for friends who didn't know him, no one to offer me sympathy.

Consequently, I feel it's time to let Nate out of the closet, with or without his consent or willingness, hoping that some other fellow will read this, think about it, and avoid the awkward situation in which I presently find myself. Loss, like joy, wants sharing.

My memories of Nate and the experiences we shared in life are fond. I am consoled by the remembrance of my own youthful fears, which Nate instinctively understood and overcame. I remain puzzled by the mystery of an unknown boy's tears. But I'm thankful, at the same time, for a long and lovely friendship, enriched by the curious enigmas of Nate's unwitting legacy.

The Unexpected Valentine

1994

Oh, that Rick! What a friend! What a guy!

I'm visiting Rick in San Francisco for three days. Jeff, our actor friend in El Lay, calls excitedly this morning to tell us he's on TV tonight, featured in a spot on a major soap opera, so I stay in to watch the show, which is scheduled for nine o'clock. It's an inconvenient time because it's impossible to go out for dinner before, and afterwards it's too late. Then, too, the timing is wrong for a real movie either before or after; consequently, one small segment of a soap opera interferes with the entire evening.

Another friend who promised to call didn't keep his promise, so I take that as an omen, in addition to feeling a certain sense of loyalty to Jeff. I decide to stay in with a book to read—even though it's the night before Valentine's Day, and I figure there will be Major Action in the streets, in the bars, in the clubs, or anywhere, despite it being a Sunday night.

At eight-thirty, Rick arrives with a spectacularly good looking fellow. Rick introduces the friend, Brad, whom he's just met at the Jackhammer, a leather bar in the Mission District. Brad is about twenty-two, six foot three, lean, with short blond hair and smooth fair skin, wearing tight jeans, no shirt, black boots, and a leather jacket. After a bit of idle chat, Rick and Brad go downstairs to Rick's Rec Room (which has become equally famous—or infamous—as Rick's Wreck Room) while I stay upstairs in the guest room with a book and TV. Rick says maybe they'll come up and watch the show, but I have my doubts, assuming they'll be otherwise engaged.

At 8:55 pm, I turn on the TV to watch the soap opera. It's completely idiotic, and Jeff's appearance lasts about two seconds. His opening moments are fine, and I watch the rest of the show, expecting he will reappear, but he doesn't. Meanwhile, Rick and

Brad are downstairs having a much better time, I'm certain, than I am. I feel I've made a mistake, both by staying in and by watching the stupid TV show, and I feel ripped off by my loyalty to Jeff. It occurs to me to telephone him and ask how much he gets paid for acting stupid on a show that's already idiotic, but I check the urge and keep my bad attitude to myself for a change.

Just after ten o'clock, there's a tap at my bedroom door. Rick is standing there, handsome, muscular, and naked except for his suntan from Costa Rica and a towel in his hand. He says, "I told Brad you'd give him a blowjob. Come on downstairs. He's waiting for you."

Incredulous, I ask, "Are you kidding?" From the look on his face, I can tell he's not kidding, so I abandon the book and take off my shirt, muttering half out-loud, "I'm not quite sure what to wear."

"You're fine! You're absolutely fine!" he assures me.

"But . . but . . .." I stammer."

"But what?" asks Rick.

"But have you finished with him?" I have to ask."

Rick smiles enigmatically and replies: "I've gone as far as I can go. Now it's up to you."

Scarcely believing my good fortune or Rick's generosity, as well as wondering what Brad's attitude might be about this whole thing, I accept the invitation, of course, telling Rick, "Thanks!"

He answers, "Thank Brad, don't thank me."

We descend the stairway and go into Rick's Rec Room. The room smells of sex and poppers. Brad is on the bed, lying on his back, naked except for a leather collar and a cock ring. His eyes are wide open, he has a delicate, slightly rococo armband tattooed on his upper arm, and his long, lean body, in complete repose, is clearly receptive.

"What a pretty picture!" I say, almost in awe.

Rick agrees, adding, "He's a beautiful man!"

Brad doesn't say anything. He doesn't have to. I sit on the edge of the bed and begin to run my fingers over Brad's tight, flat belly. Rick goes to the top of the bed near Brad's head, leans over, and begins to kiss him. Brad moans gently, and his cock begins to swell. I put my mouth on the head of it and taste a savory combination of sweat and lube. His hips began to rock under me, and as Rick kisses him and plays with his nipples, I gently begin to suck on his cock and lift his balls. Rick gives us each a hit of poppers, and the three of us begin to make love in wondrous synchronicity. As I suck on blond Brad, I can see Rick's dark cock getting bigger and bigger, and I wish I could suck on them both at the same time.

The unspoken message is to please Brad, so together Rick and I pay our separate and various attentions to Brad, who remains surprisingly recumbent and passive. Gradually, we get him, as well as ourselves, hotter and hotter. Suddenly Rick stands up and exits the room, leaving me unexpectedly alone with this tall, exquisite youth. For a moment I feel like a usurper. I'm confused, wondering, *Why am I here? How did this happen? Do I deserve this extraordinary feeling of trust? Why is Rick sharing him? Why has Rick left?*

The moment of doubt passes, and I begin simply to enjoy the feelings. Brad loves to be touched, anywhere, everywhere. His skin is flawless, his chest perfection, and his responses to my touch on his skin are almost orgasmic—so much so, I wonder what drug he might be on. I run my fingers and lips over his body, and he throbs in response. I suck on his balls and run my hands over his legs. In turn, he draws up his left leg, inviting access to his innermost parts. Slowly, gently, I put my right hand into his ass, all the while playing with his upper body and flat belly with my left hand and continuing, the whole time, to suck on his cock, which gets harder or softer in my mouth, in gradual sequences. At one point, Brad puts his left hand around his cock and begins to play with it, watching as I bite his nipples and play with the rest of his body. I put my hand in his butt once more, and he shoots his wad, wordlessly, across his flat, muscled belly. I rip off my T-shirt and underwear, grease up my dick, and masturbate on top of Brad's recumbent form as he looks up at me. Rick returns, puts his arms around me first, from behind, then hugs us both and leaves the room once again. It is reassuring and odd at the same time.

Brad still has his hand on his cock, and the sight of this beautiful man lying under me makes me crazy. I shoot off in what seems only an instant, and we lie there, close together, and with my fingertips I rub the cum into that tight, youthful body until it disappears into his skin.

Brad says, "I'm cold," and pulls the covers over him, then goes into a sleep-like trance. I get a drink of water and go upstairs to look for Rick, who is stretched out on my bed— naked, suntanned and spectacular—calmly looking at the book I had abandoned an hour or two earlier. We compare notes about Brad's astonishing beauty. Rick tells me how he first perceived Brad in the bar, bare-chested, his jacket hanging off one shoulder, tall and so incredibly stunning that no one dared approach him. Always ready for a challenge, Rick set his sights on the unknown boy, shined his magic light, and within moments they left the bar together to come back to the house for a drink and so forth.

Now it's two hours later. Rick and I agree that Brad was On Something, but neither of us can determine exactly what it was. Maybe a little pot; maybe a bit of speed, too. Probably a mixture. In any case, he's extremely high and astonishingly sensitive to touch; no doubt that's why he passed out. We go back downstairs to look at him, try to get him to talk, which he doesn't or can't, and Rick opines, not unhappily, "I think Brad's going to stay the night."

Five minutes later, much to our surprise, Brad awakens and gets up.

Each of us has a shower. We have a drink and talk for a few minutes in the kitchen. Brad doesn't have a lot to say, and it doesn't matter. I ask him why his skin is so sensitive. He smiles a slightly shy, dazzling smile, and replies ingenuously, "I guess that's something I get from my mother."

Everyone says goodnight, Rick drives Brad home, and I change the sheets, which are a mess, but that's why God invented washing machines, isn't it? Then I make up Rick's bed and leave a chocolate for him on the pillow, as at any good hotel. That's the very least he deserves.

Counting my blessings, I've determined that Rick has gone St. Valentine one better. His behavior is not exactly saintly, and he has no inclination whatsoever to become St. Rick. Nor does this have anything to do with sentimentality or sweethearts or Victoria's Secret or heart-shaped, red candy boxes. Nonetheless, Rick's generosity, charity and cleanliness are beyond, if not above, godliness, and tonight's gift was as unique, unforgettable, and spontaneous as it was—how shall I say?—deeply appreciated.

Furthermore the night before Valentine's Day is not yet over, and tomorrow night, if we choose, we have plenty of time to Go Out!

Osmosis

for Daniella Scalice
1994

This weekend a group is here at Wildwood Retreat called Foggy City Dancers. Some are playing cards in the Lodge, a few are soaking in the hot tub, and most are square-dancing in the Conference Room. A professional caller has been engaged, and the music and dancing are loud.

Tim and John, the managers and resident trustees, have both left for a few days—the first time in ten years they've felt comfortable enough to leave at the same time, given the proficiency and responsibility demonstrated by current staff. Hank, Alan the chef, and I are cooking, cleaning, washing, and serving meals—the first time we've done it alone here at Wildwood, which is a 220-acre property above the Russian River on Old Cazadero Road, which caters to a variety of people and organizations, including The Body Electric School, New Women, yoga groups, HIV retreats, and Life Coaching.

The FCD people have all been here before. They're familiar with the routines, they've brought their own music, entertainment, and bar, and they're easy to take care of—comparatively speaking.

On the other hand, the excitement of the aforementioned group is lacking. Two weeks ago, at David Morton's house party at the Ranch on Walker Creek, Chad told me he was free the following weekend, that his fiancée Daniella was going to Boston for a wedding shower for her sister. Consequently, I invited him up to Wildwood for the weekend, and everyone else began to tease us. "Who's going to be there?" they all wanted to know.

"Probably one of those New Age sexual experimentation groups," one surmised.

"No doubt," added another, "they'll engage in Tantric Sex, or something like that."

"Come on," continued a third. "Tell us all about the Tantric Sex workshops."

"Is it yoga and sex, combined?" asked another.

The ragging went on for five or ten minutes until I finally put up my hand and said, "Stop!"

Surprisingly, they stopped and waited expectantly. "Yoga, Gay Male Nudists, Body Electric, and Tantric Sex workshops are scheduled for later in the summer," I told them quietly. "This next weekend," I continued, lowering my voice confidentially, "is perhaps even more challenging than Tantric Sex." Then, with a slightly triumphal tone: "It's Firewalking."

At first, they weren't certain if they should believe me or not, but since it was the truth and because they were in the mood to expect the unexpected, they were obliged to believe it. Chad's jaw dropped in surprise, and they all wanted to know instantly if we were going to walk on fire. I explained I hadn't yet met any of the group members, that the whole thing was new for me, but I'd been told that Wildwood staff and their guests were invited to attend and participate on opening night if they so desired. Chad and I winked conspiratorially. I suggested that he leave work early so he could arrive by dinner time Friday, and that was that.

The tone was set, however, and our imaginations were seriously fired up. The following Friday, as planned, Chad arrived at sunset. We learned that the Firewalkers' opening ceremony was set for the following night, Saturday, and that an afternoon preparation conference and ritual would precede the actual fire lighting and fire walk. The week had been intense; Chad and I were both tired. After dinner we gave each other backrubs and went to sleep, hoping for a long hike the next day before the fire walking event.

Saturday morning dawned cold, gray, and rainy. We ate breakfast, read, and listened to music, and I did my chores. We were both disappointed, but there was nothing to do but wait and hope the weather would change, as it frequently does. By noon, however, it seemed that the storm had completely settled in, and I tried to think of something else we could do that would be amusing. Chad had driven all the way from Santa Cruz, and we both had anticipated doing something exciting—all the more since it was the first time in almost a year that I'd seen him without Daniella, and given that several of our previous weekends and trips together had been sensational. Our spirits were not dampened by the rain, but we did voice some concern about whether a fire walk would be possible in the storm.

Seized by a sudden inspiration, I telephoned Osmosis Enzyme Baths in Freestone, a place I'd heard about but never visited. It was explained that the procedure included the following: first, herbal tea in a secluded Japanese garden, followed by immersion in an enzyme bath assisted by a female attendant, then a brushing off and shower, concluding with a half-hour blanket wrap. The enzyme bath, we were told, consisted of tubs filled with aromatic cedar chips, bran mulch, and enzymes which, like compost, created natural heat because of a chemical reaction. Slightly skeptical, but with no real alternative, we made an appointment for two-thirty in the afternoon.

After lunch, impatient for something to happen, we left early, drove down to the Russian River, along the Bohemian Highway to the little town of Occidental, and went for a walk in the rain. As if by magic, a flotilla of ancient automobiles arrived, evidently a club of vintage vehicle enthusiasts who had braved the rain to meet for lunch at a popular restaurant. We examined flawless 1932 and 1934 Packards, three or four Cords from the mid-thirties (Chad had never even heard of a Cord automobile!), a convertible, a coupe, and two four-door models. Cadillacs from 1947, another Packard from the early '50s, a 1966 Corvette—all in perfect condition, of course—and a brand-new Ferrari, as well as a couple of ancient vehicles which we were unable to identify, each of them almost as large as a locomotive, especially in contrast to the modern, compact Japanese, European and American cars parked in the restaurant lot adjacent.

We drove on toward Bodega Bay, visited a well-stocked, attractive antique shop, and suddenly it was time to race back to Freestone for our appointment. From the moment we drove into the parking space at Osmosis, we knew something special was taking place. The landscaping promised both order and symmetry of a high level, and the building, which at first appeared to be a piece of architectural fantasy from a cowboy movie, turned out to be a sophisticated, beautifully composed and constructed Country-Japanese-influenced design fitted into a nineteenth-century Western structure, creating an unusual ensemble unlike anything else anywhere. We left our shoes under a bench on the front porch, said hello to an extremely vocal, sculptural black cat, signed in at the registry, and were introduced to our personal attendant, Laura, a soft-spoken, serious young woman with short dark hair and lovely skin unencumbered by makeup, who ushered us into an austerely furnished, superbly harmonious, Japanese-style room overlooking a garden, pond, and bridge of astonishing esthetic style, grace, and sheer magical beauty. Without pretension, everything was perfect in its way.

Japanese flute music played softly in the background, and Laura served us aromatic herb tea in small porcelain cups. She explained the bath procedure, invited us to relax and suggested we stroll in the garden. Not a leaf was out of place. Plants, shrubs, bonsai, and flowers were arranged in elegant precision. Having tested the mosses, admired the garden from different angles, and perceived a most unusual plant which appeared to be blossoming underwater, we returned inside for another cup of tea, and, as if on cue from central casting, the black cat, accompanied by another sculptural cat which was the color of variegated fine woods, paraded and posed throughout the perfect garden. Except for the soft music and the delicate drip of a bamboo fountain, we heard no intrusive or unwelcome sounds. Overhead the heavens gradually began to lighten, and as we watched, pale blue skies and scudding white clouds replaced the soggy, leaden morning storm.

Laura returned with neck pillows: padded, heated, shaped, collar devices which were both warm and aromatic as well as slightly weighted. Because the day had been particularly cold and rainy, the weight, scent, and warmth of these neck pillows was unusually comforting. Once again, the idea of the device was simple, yet neither of us had experienced anything like it. We sipped our tea, lulled by the warmth of our neck halos and relaxed by the placid atmosphere and herbal tea.

After an appropriate interval of relaxation, we were invited to a dressing room where we left our clothing in lockers and selected one each from a variety of kimonos. Laura then took us into a large room fitted with rectangular, redwood tubs, not unlike coffins, each filled with a rich loamy substance, a mixture as previously described of cedar shavings, bran mulch, and aromatics, all of which had been treated with enzymes to produce a chemical heat reaction. Laura hollowed out places for us in two adjacent tubs, we removed our kimonos, and climbed in naked. The sensation was unique, peculiar but not unpleasant, and we gradually settled in, covering ourselves with the wood mixture. Laura then built up the areas under our necks and gradually loaded more and more of the mixture over our bodies, so that we could feel the weight of the loam as well as the heat. The feeling was extraordinarily pleasant, and the scents of the heated herbs contributed to an overall sense of remarkable well-being.

When we felt completely comfortable, Laura opened an enormous picture window, previously clouded by steam, which made up almost half of the wall. The tubs looked out over another Japanese garden, suddenly in focus, this one more austere, with a floor of raked stones interrupted by large, well-placed viewing rocks and lacey trees.

White, puffy clouds chased rainclouds across the sky. While immersed in the aromatic loam, we watched the play of the ever-changing cloudscape, still enjoying cool air on our exposed faces while simultaneously experiencing profound, overall warmth.

So overcome were we by the extraordinary combination of sensual, visual, and aromatic pleasures that conversation seemed superfluous, and we barely spoke for the twenty or so minutes of immersion. Laura visited twice, with cold water to drink and cold compresses to press against our foreheads. When it came time to leave the tubs, the feeling was a semblance of primeval man emerging from primordial ooze. The casings first began to crumble as we moved fingers and toes, then gradually—and, in fact, reluctantly—we crawled out of the shavings, emerging with the aspect of incomplete, humanoid, reddish-brown sculptures composed of a peculiarly grainy terra cotta. Brushes were provided, as well as an outdoor deck, and we brushed ourselves and each other in what seemed a curiously atavistic ritual before taking showers in adjoining stalls which were both meticulously clean and miraculously modern, especially in comparison to what had seemed a ritually primitive, soul-fulfilling cleansing to rid us of ordinary life and times.

When dry, we once again donned kimonos and were taken into a dimly lit room furnished only with futons on the floor. Wrapped with warm blankets and encased with another warmed, aromatic neck pillow, each of us was draped from head to toe, fitted with a headset, and left to dream and doze in an alpha state for the next half hour or so.

The procedure completed, we returned to the dressing room and slowly put on our normal clothing. Glowing, in a wonderful mood—literally "full of wonder"—we walked out onto the porch and put on our shoes to step back into what passes for Real Life, but not before Chad encountered an old friend from school, arriving at Osmosis with her boyfriend. Since neither had been there before, they were both surprised and pleased at the coincidence of meeting in such an unlikely locale.

Remarking once again the subtle beauty of the landscaping, we also noticed the storm had completely passed and the sun had come out, so on the spot we decided to drive back to Wildwood to embark on a sunset hike. We put the top down, turned up the heat, and drove back through some of the most beautiful redwood groves remaining on the planet. We talked about what a splendidly unplanned, beautiful, unusual, and exciting day had occurred; how lucky we had been to avoid sinking into depression on account of the rain, and how extraordinary it is that something unusual happens whenever we get together.

What we didn't know or realize, at that point, was that our extraordinary day was simply a prelude to an equally extraordinary evening.

Back at Wildwood, we parked the car, filled a backpack with water, dried fruits, a small flask of Scotch, a pocketknife, and sweaters. The firewalkers were planning dinner early to accommodate the ritual preceding their evening ceremony, but Chad and I decided to enjoy our hike instead, departing just after five o'clock.

We each dropped a tab of LSD at the beginning of the hike, carefully hoarded and saved for just such a rare occasion. The air was sharp with ozone, and the path through the forest magical. Wild iris, Scotch broom, and small flowers dotted the ground, and mosses on the trees seemed thicker, denser, and more brilliant than usual. Grasses had been cleansed and dampened by the rain, and leaves glistened in the raking late afternoon sunlight. Once across the stream, we stopped to rest in the meadow, and a shaft of sunshine, as if from a spotlight, outlined the meadow and limned Chad's figure indelibly into my brain. It was one of those rare days that I decided not to carry the camera, since we had departed so late, and of course I wished I could have captured even a fragment of the moment on film, but it was not to be.

Below the knoll on which we were resting, Lady, Wildwood's horse, suddenly appeared. Chad had not known a horse was on the property and was at first somewhat startled. I began to talk to Lady, told her there were no apples in the pack today, but that she might like to try a dried peach. She watched, unmoving, for a few minutes, while I explained to Chad that Lady and I had a game, and that if I moved towards her, she would meet me halfway. He didn't really believe me, but I moved towards her, and sure enough, she met me halfway. I opened the pack and tentatively gave her a dried peach, which she ate with alacrity. We petted her, talked to her, and she kept trying to get back into the pack. We sat down on the ground, and she stood over us, trying to find something else to eat. Because there wasn't anything else, she made do with grass, and we had the peculiar experience of watching a horse eat from a vantage point underneath her muzzle. Before leaving the meadow, we gave her a few additional dried peaches and continued our hike.

The light was magical; sunset lingered on longer than usual, as if to make up for the dreary beginning of the day. By the time we began to head back, it was getting dark, and I realized I'd never been on the Wildwood trails at night. It wasn't frightening—on the contrary, it was an adventure. Besides, we had a flashlight and a flask of Scotch. As we climbed, however, the trail became blacker and blacker, and at one point I feared we'd lost the path. We stopped, reconnoitered, and discussed our plight. We redescended somewhat, determined we were indeed on the right path, and continued upwards once again, until a familiar fencepost assured us that we were, in fact, not lost. A little further on, we stopped at a carved log nicknamed "The Bus Stop." Extremely relieved at not being lost, I told Chad that no one must ever know that I even considered the possibility that we were lost. It would be far too embarrassing to admit it since it's assumed I know what I'm doing around here.

As the path climbed, more and more moonlight pierced the canopy of trees, and at a certain height, electric lights in the far distance became apparent. Just below the point denoting the edge of the property, we remembered that the firewalkers might be in process of their ceremony and that it was important for us to be quiet as well as respectful.

An eerie glow became visible through the trees, and a Gothic blast of moonlight shot out from behind a cloud. The glow flickered, trees beneath the point were outlined by an enormous fire, yet we could hear nothing. Proceeding cautiously, we moved toward the point, and as we rounded the path at the edge of the clearing, we perceived a lone figure carrying a glowing wand, dancing around the edge of a bonfire. Sparks were flying into the air, into the trees, and into the wind. As a native who has survived several California wildfires, it appeared extremely dangerous to me.

The figure, interspersed between the flames, silhouettes of the trees, and flashes of moonlight, alternating with dark, scudding clouds, appeared to be something out of a Japanese medieval illustration. The sacred, pagan nature of both dance and setting were completely compelling. We stopped in our tracks, mesmerized by the dancer and the flames. Slowly and gradually we approached the fire, as though it were a temple, realizing only at the last moment that the shaman or priest figure was Arthur, a group member who had arrived the day before with his wife, Charlotte. Arthur was tending the fire and Charlotte was off fetching more wood. Arthur explained that the group was still in the conference room, they'd be down shortly, and he invited us to stay. Because we had missed dinner, we were hungry and decided to first eat something and then return to the fire, the point, the dancer, and the group.

Back at the lodge, all was quiet. Staff had retired and guests were in the conference room above the pool. Alan had left out two plates, each a dinner wrapped in plastic, with our names, a most thoughtful and considerate gesture. We opened a bottle of wine, sat in the darkened lodge, and mused over the five hours we had spent since returning from the enzyme baths. Already it had been quite a day, and we both knew that it wasn't over. Magical energy was in the atmosphere, which couldn't be denied.

We walked back to the point where Arthur and Charlotte were tending and renewing the fire, and only moments after our arrival there, we heard drumming followed by voices, and gradually a group of twenty-five or thirty people proceeded onto the clearing around the fire. Some of the people were beating drums, some were playing percussion instruments, and a few old hippies (I thought to myself, critically) were playing tambourines.

The sacred nature of the place and moment seemed transformed by cheap theatrics, and Chad and I glanced at each other in dismay, surprised by the tawdry quality of the introduction to something we had considered supremely spiritual. Several members of the group were photographing the fire along with the participants with flash cameras, which seemed even more crass than the tambourines.

The conference leader, a buxom blonde called Peggy, invited everyone to stand around the fire and make contact with it. She asked people first to play with the fire, and various individuals began to run around the flames and jump over them. When initial moves had been completed, she asked everyone present to make a circle and hold hands. The group complied, the moon emerged from behind a cloud, and like a pagan high priestess from some other time and place, Peggy raised her hands and invoked the spirits of the earth, fire, sky, and water. The moment became intensely religious, the ritual became completely serious, and I felt an almost out-of-body experience, not knowing what country or what century I was in.

Later on, Chad felt something similar, saying: "If this had happened in some other place, in a different language, in some distant culture, it would be easier to believe—but it's here, in our country, in California, in English. It's not easy to believe this can be happening here and now, even though it's right in front of us."

Following the incantation, Peggy invited group members to each take turns with a rake, to personally make contact with the fire, raking the mixture and transforming the bonfire into a large, rectangular bed of glowing coals. When the bed was relatively flat, she invited and encouraged those who were ready to walk across the glowing rectangle. Some of those present removed their shoes and socks, and with no further ado began to run, dance, and walk over the coals. It was startling to watch at first. They seemed to experience no pain, and it was clear that their feet weren't blistered. We watched in astonishment as people crossed the coals sometimes singly, sometimes together. Several ran, some twirled or pirouetted, and others simply walked across very slowly. Having crossed once, each returned to cross in a different spot or at a different pace.

We had noticed that Alan had come out to watch and was on the opposite side of the circle. We moved around to join him, and by the time we arrived he was beginning to take off his shoes and socks, clearly in preparation to walk. Chad and I looked at each other, knowing it was now or never, and with no further discussion we too removed our shoes and socks quickly. The three of us took each other's hands and walked across the rectangle of coals, all together. The first time we crossed rather quickly, and once arrived on the other side, realizing that we had done it and it hadn't hurt, we returned and crossed again, slowly and separately this time.

We did it! We walked on fire! The realization was almost anti-climactic. As everyone put on his or her shoes and socks, a woman from the group came over with a worried expression and asked, "Are you fellows all right?" to which we replied: "Of course!"

She continued, "Everyone who met with us beforehand signed a release, so I have to make sure that you're all right and that you're not going to sue us or anything like that."

Laughing, we assured her we were in fine shape, and shortly after that, when Peggy invited everyone to return to the conference room to discuss their experiences, we felt it behooved us to accompany them and participate somewhat more than we had beforehand.

The debriefing was generally quite lighthearted. Everyone was high from the experience, and the group mood was elevated, although the recitations of each person's impressions and feelings were more down-to-earth than exalted. Peggy reiterated what had evidently been discussed during the afternoon meetings: that firewalking is not an end in itself but a metaphor for conquering fears of any sort, and that what one learns is to confront fear—in this case fear of fire—and then conquer it with no harmful consequences. Once learned, this technique can be used in other contexts to transform one's life.

Chad and I returned to our room transformed. Because we've done something few twentieth-century "civilized" men or women have done, we're unable to remain the same as we were before. And it happened magically, as if by osmosis.

Holiday Recipe

for Dr. David Richards

2000

This morning I decided to begin preparations for Thanksgiving dinner by cooking the huge pumpkin which has been out on the deck since Halloween. When I carried it into the kitchen, it appeared even larger than it did outside, and of course it wouldn't fit into the oven. While contemplating the issue, it occurred to me the best thing to do was saw the pumpkin into smaller pieces. That suddenly reminded me of a true story an English friend related to me some years ago, which I never wrote down. Here's the recipe:

First you take a struggling medical student living in London, who has on a whim decided to invite ten friends to Christmas dinner. Realizing you have no money to buy a traditional goose, you chance on the brilliant idea of poaching a swan from Her Majesty's Pond, which you pass frequently to and from medical school.

Consequently, in the dead of night, you complete your sordid task and take the dead bird back to your tiny flat, where you learn two things: first, the flesh of a swan is black, and secondly, the fowl is more than twice as large as your oven.

Then, utilizing your recently honed surgical skills, you cut the bird into six pieces, hoping to cook at least two pieces at a time in the unfortunate oven. Dismayed almost to tears by the complications of the procedure, you decide to go out to the local gay pub and drown your frustrations in a pint or two.

You meet an attractive fellow there whom you chat up for a possible assignation. You casually inform him you're a medical student and ask him what he's doing professionally in London. To your utmost chagrin, he tells you he is Keeper of Her Majesty's Swans, which causes you to turn pale and flee the pub with no further conversation. Back in the flat, you take hold of yourself and think what to do next, and it's surprisingly simple. You borrow an enormous soup-pot from a neighbor, then poach the uncooked meat, smiling at the glorious, ultimate irony of serving your Christmas guests Twice-Poached Swan.

One Regret
2004

George had everything: looks, fortune, intelligence, talent and
brilliance. As a young man, he was a champion yachtsman
and skier. Blessed with an aristocratic bearing, charm, and an
Icelandic heritage, he was the prototypical Aryan: tall, blond,
fair-skinned, and subject to frequent suffering from sunburn.
To alleviate this troublesome problem, which interfered with his
sailing and skiing, he invented the world's first sunburn preven-
tative lotion, a product he called "SKOL." The tanning lotion
became a chemical company, which evolved into a series of
chemical companies. George's companies grew and prospered so
that he was able to purchase a splendid house on a private island
just outside Miami, a town house in Manhattan, and a magnificent 2,500-acre farm in Vermont. That was in 1935, when 2,500
acres with a small farmhouse, could be bought for $35,000. That
was also just six years after the Crash of '29, when $35,000 was
equivalent to a million dollars or more in today's paper money.

By the time I met George and his lover Terry, the small
Vermont farmhouse had become an architectural Cape Dutch
masterpiece, with surrounding grounds a landscaping feat of
equal distinction. The house by then was transformed into a
mansion with Dutch dormers, a gabled roof, fireplaces in every
room, plus bedrooms and baths to accommodate a dozen guests
in luxury. The surrounding compound, which included a barn
and an additional house for staff, accommodated a couple,
Mary & Jim Merchant, who cared for the property all year
long. Jim cared for the grounds, livestock and dogs, while Mary
cleaned, cooked, and kept house for George, Terry and their
guests during the summer months and at Christmastime, the
only times of year George chose to avail himself of the Farm.

As luck would have it—and George's unfailing luck was
exceptional—a talc mine was discovered on the Vermont

property, and over the years revenues from talc mining provided wherewithal for additions and transformations of the terrain as well as the buildings. Two lakes were created, one adjacent to the main house and another in the hills about a mile from the house. A cabin was added to the more remote lakes, then a gazebo, a walled kitchen garden, a bell tower, an antique weathervane, a tree-lined allée, and other amenities came to grace an already graceful landscape.

Furnished with antique furniture and silver, decorated with Persian carpets and artworks of great beauty as well as excellent quality, the house developed a patina of elegance, refinement, and charm rare to find anywhere, but especially rare in the far reaches of the Northeast.

In December of 1969, my dear friend Dorothy returned from a prolonged sojourn in Europe. En route to California, she stopped to visit me in Boston just before Christmastime, where I chanced to be house and dog-sitting for friends who were out of town. Surprised that I had no plans for Christmas, she announced, "We will visit George and Terry in Vermont," and got right on the phone.

George, she related to me subsequently, said, "We would love to see you, but we have an absolute rule not to invite anyone we don't know already to the Farm at Christmastime." "Nonsense," retorted Dorothy. "You will all love each other, and we'll be there the day after tomorrow."

"Dorothy," I said nervously, as she got off the phone, "there's one other thing."

"What's that, darling?" she asked.

"The dogs," I replied. "I can't leave them here." With a wave of her arm, she announced: "That's no problem. We'll bring them along!"

So that was that. Two days later, Dorothy, the two Corgis, Artemis & Antiope, and I were loaded into the car, along with winter coats, gloves, mufflers, a bottle of rum, and a thermos of hot tea. The drive to Vermont was snow-covered, lovely, magical, and Dorie related to me the story of how she had met George and Terry several years earlier. George had taken a house in St. Paul de Vence and left Terry there, ostensibly to study French, while he made a tour of his European business operations. At the time Dorothy happened to be learning French at the same international school as Terry. George, who was then in his middle fifties, had met Terry only a year previously, and Terry was then eighteen. Their relationship was intense as well as passionate, despite the difference in their ages, and when Terry turned twenty-one, George adopted him legally and officially. They subsequently traveled as father and son—a clever ploy in the conservative 1950s and '60s.

The driveway to Reading Farms is about a mile long, and the first view of the compound, across snow-covered fields and the lake capped with ice, is like coming upon a phantasmagorical, northern European Christmas card. As we drove up to the house, Mary Merchant, George's long-time housekeeper, came out to greet us. As soon as the car doors opened, the Corgis jumped out, licked Mary's hand, and we were thenceforth assured a permanent place in her own personal heaven, which turned out to be a good thing for us all, dogs as well as humans. George, tall, elegant, and silver-haired, greeted us warmly, and any reservations he entertained about our arrival were never for a single instant exhibited. Terry, then twenty-five, was a complete and total charmer: handsome, lively, intelligent, well-built, athletic, personable and undeniably sexy. Dorothy and I were installed in separate, glorious bedroom suites: Dorie's with a canopy bed, and mine with a Palladian window overlooking a lake. Tea was served adjacent to a roaring fire in the library, and within moments, whatever doubts anyone might have had were forever dispelled. That day a tradition, as well as a lasting friendship, was born, and every Christmas subsequent, until George's death four years later, and for another six years after that, I was honored and delighted to be a regular guest at The Farm, for a week or two in August and always at Christmastime.

Mary proved to be not only an excellent cook, but a veritable gold mine of information. My habit was to wake early in the morning, and over coffee with Mary in the kitchen, I learned who was who, what had happened, who had done what mischief to whom, who was a saint, who was a devil, and most of the legends of Reading Farms. As far as I was concerned, George was the supreme legend, and one of the men whom I would emulate, if I could, then or now. By the time other guests had descended for proper breakfast—not in the kitchen and not in the dining room, but in a specially built, east-facing room with yellow walls and an ancient Swedish porcelain furnace—a flood of morning light complemented Mary's copious breakfasts and wondrous array of silver serving salvers to set off the Royal Copenhagen china. Little by little, I discovered exactly what was going on, because Mary knew everything. Yet there was a coy pretense, established many years before. Terry's room adjoined George's, and even though they slept together and had done for years, Terry always rumpled the bed in his own room, out of deference to Mary's supposed delicacy about such matters. I suppose it was a matter of as much merriment to her as it was to them.

During the last few months of his life, rendered uncomfortable by a rapidly advancing cancer, George was also concerned about losses sustained by a Belgian subsidiary of his company. Unable to travel or to deal with that problem, he became concerned for Terry's sake. Worrying that Terry might not be able to deal with the financial difficulties, on his deathbed George married a woman whom he had known for many years. Because she was even wealthier than George, he mistakenly thought she would assist Terry financially as well as emotionally, following his demise. George's judgment, at the time, was uncharacteristically impaired, and the woman in question, almost immediately following George's death, did her best to seize George's properties and assets, despite an ironclad will. Terry, much to his credit, remained generous in his understanding and treatment of her, despite her despicable behavior. The problems created by this woman's avarice were not resolved for two years, but Terry never sank to her level, never spoke ill of her, and remained optimistic that George's will and his own rights would be respected.

During this period of mourning, transition, difficulty, and compromise, Terry scaled down enormously. He sold the big house in Miami, moved to a small apartment, sold the town house in Manhattan, and vowed to keep the farm in Vermont. Taking a firm hold of the business, he successfully sold off the unprofitable subsidiary, remained patient until the problems with George's deathbed widow were solved, and triumphed in keeping The Farm. It became clear to everyone that George had chosen well, that he had taken the raw clay of a promising, although uneducated, young man, and with patience as well as the wisdom of his heart combined with his years of experience, created and molded the son he desired from the boy he loved. And Terry, as George's son and heir, fulfilled his own potential.

Meanwhile, George had been everywhere and done everything. Not only that, but he'd done it all First Class, with style, flair, élan; he remembered all the people, all the places and all the names. He had a fantastic memory and was a virtuoso raconteur. With wit, sparkle, and touches of nostalgia, he evoked and personified a pre-war world of elegance and glamour, the likes of which none of us will see again: Berlin and Paris in the twenties, Budapest and Rome in the thirties, Havana in the forties, yacht races in the Pacific, ski championships in the Alps, an early marriage followed by an early divorce, various liaisons after the breakup of his marriage, his ex-wife's subsequent marriage to a gangster, gay encounters before the word "gay" existed, endless synchronicities and eccentricities of a life which seemed itself a picaresque novel in the living as well as in the recounting of it.

Mary's elegant dinners at The Farm were always served by candlelight – an unusual amount of candlelight, which emanated from a pair of unique, 17th century Irish candelabra distinguished by their enormous height as well as by their flexibility. These could be utilized individually or together, and the arms of each could be moved so that they might be placed in a round or flat juxtaposition with each other. They were so tall they never interfered with sight lines across the dining table. They cast a remarkable, soft glow from above, enhancing the appearance of everyone lucky enough to be present. Mary's service was not exactly unobtrusive, and her pithy comments were as much a part of the meals at Reading Farms as her extraordinary desserts. Mary thought a *crème brûlée*, for example, incomplete unless it was served with an angel cake, and George seldom served a wine which had not been properly decanted beforehand.

Cocktails were served in various locations depending on the season: the gazebo or garden outside when it was warm enough, and the library when the weather cooled down. Following dinner, guests customarily retired to the library for coffee, cognac, and a fireside chat. One such evening, during which George had regaled us with yet another masterful tale, I remarked, "George, your life has been extraordinary. You've gone everywhere in the world, you've done everything and everyone possible, you've known everyone important, and everything you touched turned to gold. Your life seems to have been completely charmed, and I'd like to know if there's anything you haven't done, or if there's anything you regret."

George smiled ruefully for a fraction of a second, paused only to heighten the drama of the moment, and replied: "Yes, in fact, there is one thing I regret. Something that came about just when I was buying The Farm in the mid-thirties. I was offered a European title—an Italian title, it was, for a certain price. Unlike the English or the French, the Italians are more businesslike, more pragmatic, with their titles, and this one became available. I remember thinking at the time that it was a bit silly, as well as unnecessarily pretentious, to have a title, and I turned down the offer. Later I came to regret that decision because . . . you see . . . I could have become the Count of Monte Cristo."

Breakfast in Alexandria

2007

It was the day before Thanksgiving. My partner thom and I had come downstairs for breakfast with our host, Will, in Alexandria, Virginia. Will had invited twenty-five people the previous evening for a cocktail party in honor of our visit to the Washington, D.C., area. Coffee was already brewed, and Will was busy in the kitchen putting together a grand assemblage of fruit salad, smoked salmon, breads, cheeses, and other delicacies remaining from the previous evening's celebrations. A white tablecloth covered the breakfast table, along with all the silver. Will explained that he's a Big Southern Queen, in case we hadn't noticed.

In an expansive mood, with the strain of preparing for the party behind, Will was almost giddy with excitement, and he had detailed dish about the guests: who had been dating whom, who moved away, who failed to show up, who looked good and who didn't. The usual after-party deconstruction.

Interspersed with these mini-conversations were snippets about Will's past, his parents and grandparents, his Southern upbringing, his childhood in Virginia, his uncle and grandfather who both committed suicide. Their lifelong smoking habits had resulted in emphysema for them to such an extent that, unable to breathe, they had separately decided and succeeded in blowing out their brains.

Not in the best of health himself, Will had kept himself alive with home renovation projects, travels abroad, and collections of antique furniture, silver, and glassware, mostly from the 1820s and 1830s. Tall and fair, with red-blond hair beginning to gray, Will, in his graceful, lanky way, epitomized a grownup "southern boy." Since we'd visited him three years earlier, he'd redone his home in Alexandria, just across the Potomac River from Washington, D.C., adding a grand stairway leading from a new entry into both a lofty dining room on the main floor and to a light-filled guestroom and bath on the second floor. He expanded the kitchen inside and added an exterior garden room, which in bug season, by the touch of a button, becomes instantly enclosed with screens. Will, like a five-year-old with a new toy, derived great joy in demonstrating this feature.

Garrulous, generous, and good-natured, Will had a bit of trouble finishing sentences. His mind flitted around constantly, and before he finished one thought, another had crowded it from his consciousness. The resulting array of phrases was a rapid-fire delivery, leaping from rock to rock, and subject to subject, in a virtual torrent of verbal ejaculations.

Will's dog, Wayne, was the center of his household. Wayne, a big old furry spaniel barked furiously whenever someone arrived or departed, and otherwise sat or lay around quietly awaiting attention and affection. Thom and I decided Wayne replaced Will's partner, Roger, who died a dozen years ago.

Will brought photos to the breakfast table, talking all the while and showing us first images of Roger, whom we never knew, and then of Wayne at ten months. At one point, reminded of his grandmother, he returned to tales of his Southern Gothic upbringing, which led to a neighbor of his uncle's in the Virginia countryside. This neighbor with two names, Billy Joe, had a wife who became mysteriously ill, and she spent several years in consultation with various doctors. It was eventually determined she had contracted a venereal disease previously known only in pigs, and the trail of infection led to Billy Joe, who ultimately confessed to fucking his pig. The story became major local gossip—front page news, in fact. The unfortunate and disgraced wife divorced Billy Joe and fled with her two children, while Billy Joe was tried, convicted for bestiality, and forced to languish in jail for his sins. The more unfortunate pig, Will told us, was shot and killed for his.

At this, Will jumped up from the table, ran into his study, and returned with a small box. Opening it triumphantly, he pulled out a toy—a petite white pig with a pale little naked man behind it sporting a bright-red, oversized phallus. Will cranked the miniature wheel on the side of the toy causing the little man to begin fucking the pig at remarkable speed, and we all began to roar with laughter.

"Where on earth did you get that?" I asked him. "In Virginia? Is this a twisted Southern toy?"

"No," he replied. "It's from China!" Then he treated us to a second display, almost as funny as the first. "Here," he continued, putting it back in the box and handing it to me, "I'm giving it to you. It really belongs in California, so you have to take it back with you."

"I'm honored," was my reply. "No one has ever given me a pig-fucking sculpture before, nor do I know anyone who has ever discussed the subject at breakfast!"

The Archdeacon's Birthday

2013

The program for Evensong at Grace Cathedral read: "Tonight's Evensong honors the birthday of the Venerable Anthony Turney, Deacon for the Arts."

We arrived fifteen minutes early and were directed by a small, printed sign informing us that guests were welcome to sit in the Quire. I had attended a few services, memorials, and concerts at the Cathedral in San Francisco, but had never previously sat in the Quire. Our friend Otis, a retired Bishop, attired in high clerical garb, had saved seats for four of us in the last row of the Quire.

These seats were adjacent to the organ console and keyboard, while the organ pipes flanked the Quire on both sides of opposing rows of benches. The organist, in a white surplice with a long academic hood on the back, arrived with his scores and began the Voluntary, a Bach hymn, as the procession entered. To my amazement and great pleasure, the pipes directly opposite were creating a remarkably clear and beautiful sound. Each note and chiff of the pipes as they opened were discernible, and the overall effect much less muddled than the sound one hears in the Nave. And when the thirty-two-foot pipes were engaged, the rumble and sound were literally palpable.

The proximity of the instrument reminded me of my year of baroque music study at the Amsterdam Conservatory. I was learning harpsichord and organ repertoire, and my teacher and mentor, Gustav Leonhardt, was not only a superb harpsichordist and teacher; he was also principal organist for the Oude Kerk, the oldest church in the City. He was frequently invited to perform at other churches throughout the Netherlands and was generous enough to invite his students to accompany him, visit the ancient churches, attend rehearsals and have an opportunity to play some of the greatest baroque organs in the world—at Zwolle, Haarlem, and, of course, in Amsterdam.

In returning to the United States, it seemed the best of instruments in local churches could not compete with the great seventeenth and eighteenth century tracker-action instruments of Holland or Germany, and I seldom managed much enthusiasm for recent American electronic instruments. Therefore, it was a pleasant surprise to be seated in the direct path of a splendid set of pipes.

The procession included two Lesson readers, preceded by a Ceremonial Verger carrying his "verge," all wearing purple vestments. The Choir of Men and Boys, preceded by a youth in a white surplice guiding a group of young boys in purple robes, all took their places on benches. The guests in attendance stood as the procession entered, and I realized this was not a simple presentation of a few hymns but rather a High Church Invitatory and Psalter; consequently, tall candles were ceremoniously lit as the procession advanced and the guest of honor was seated.

Opening Sentences were pronounced followed by Preces and a hymn in which the choir and all guests were requested to participate. A Psalm was sung by the choir alone, and The Lessons followed, with a reading from Isaiah, a Magnificat by Orlando Gibbons, The Nunc Dimittis, and The Apostles' Creed. Subsequently came The Prayers, The Lord's Prayer, The Suffrages, The Collects, an anthem, and Closing Prayers, followed by another hymn and voluntary.

The Bishop, several deans, and various colleagues delivered encomiums to Anthony and his long service to the Cathedral, as well as to the community at large and to the nation. The esteem in which he is held was apparent and the ceremonies thoughtful, considerate, and appropriate.

The entire program lasted just under an hour, following which everyone was invited to a reception in the Chapter House adjacent. As guests filed out of the Nave and across the Courtyard, the carillonneur was performing "Happy Birthday," my least favorite and the most overplayed song in the world. For once, it made me smile to hear it spread over Nob Hill from the mighty bells in the Cathedral's Singing Tower.

The solemnity of the service over, I was waxing eloquent about the sounds of the organ from up close and remarked quietly to my husband thom that the music was a sort of divine blowjob. What could be more perfect for an Anglican birthday bash?

With Love and Kisses from Charlie

for Sean Strub and Charlie Beye
2014

My friend Sean Strub recently wrote and published a powerful memoir, not only of his life, but of a time during which the world changed drastically, especially for gay men. His book, entitled *Body Counts: A Memoir of Politics, AIDS, Sex, and Survival* received rave reviews, which it richly deserves.

Sean was in San Francisco a few weeks ago to give readings, book signings, and interviews with the press. He was our houseguest during that time and so busy we saw little of him, which was not unexpected.

Today he sent me an email, addressed to him, which he was gracious enough to forward. It has occurred to me that if we were in a previous century, this would have been an epistolary correspondence which may have taken weeks, if not months. Now it happens in moments, and all of this transpired in one day.

Let's begin with the email Sean received and forwarded to me:

On Apr 4, 2014, at 7:51 AM, Sean Strub wrote:

Angus,
Forwarded with Charlie's permission. If you haven't read his memoir, My Husband and My Wives, I recommend it.
xxSOS

\-\-\-\-\-\-\-\-\- Forwarded message \-\-\-\-\-\-\-\-\-\-
From: Charles Beye <chuckbeye@comcast.net>
Date: Thu, Apr 3, 2014 at 10:24 PM
Subject: your memoir
To: Sean Strub <sean.strub@gmail.com>

dear sean, that is quite a book, and i was glad to read it, and revisit the horror stories of those years as well as the many positive aspects of all that extraordinary resistance to what seemed the inevitable. how wonderful that your health has improved so. and that you have memories of many good emotional relationships as well as the sustained pride in turning out that great magazine. in reading the acknowledgement i came across the name of angus whyte. i had not thought of him in years. once a long time ago at a party in cambridge which i attended with my then wife, at which the majority of the guests were university faculty, mostly straight, and if gay, then understood to be so, but not as a rule acknowledged as such by their peers, hosted by an elderly jewish fag hag art historian who was always upset by any reference to gayness of any sort, as my wife and i were leaving, and the middle of the room was somewhat deserted, and my wife had preceded me toward the exit, angus came over and i stretched out my hand to bid him adieu and he took me in his arms powerfully yet gently and kissed me deep and full with an open mouth for a dramatic length of time, to which habit and instinct let me respond although another part of my psyche said: "charlie, don't do it." best wishes, Charlie

Not having heard anything from or about Charlie for almost forty years, I was stunned to read this email, and decided to reply to Sean immediately, as follows:

Dear Sean,

What a lovely message! And what a surprise!!

To tell the truth, I had not thought of Charlie for a long time, and it's been 37 years since I moved away from Boston. I didn't know he had written a book, and he probably didn't know that I wrote one either.

Thanks for forwarding me his message, and I will send him a note shortly.

What a reputation I had in those days! (In NYC at a party at the Dakota in the early '70's at Mendy Wager's apartment, I was introduced to a handsome young man, who exclaimed: "Angus Whyte! I've heard of you!" to which I queried: "And just what did you hear, may I ask?" And his response was: "You give the best parties, and you know the cutest boys.")

I found that to be an excellent reputation.

Love,

XXAngus

Then I wrote an email to Charlie, as well:

On Apr 4, 2014, at 12:39 PM, Angus Whyte <anguswhyte@mac.com> wrote:

Dear Charlie,

I have just received and read this very sweet message from Sean, and here's my reply to him. I look forward to reading your book, and I'm attaching the poster image for mine, which came out a year ago.

Hoping you are well and thriving, where are you now and what are you doing?

After ten years in L.A. during the eighties, I moved to France to renovate a seven hundred year old tower in the Périgord. My plan was to stay there and renovate old places for Americans and Germans who didn't speak French, but after I completed the work on the tower, which cost four times what I had anticipated, the Big Recession following the Gulf War torpedoed my plans, and I unwillingly returned to San Francisco, where I still am.

Sending you a big, open-mouthed cyber kiss, I look forward to an update.

Aloha,

Angus

Begin forwarded message:

From: Charles Beye <chuckbeye@comcast.net>

Subject: Re: your memoir

Date: April 4, 2014 9:57:20 AM PDT

To: Angus Whyte <anguswhyte@mac.com>

oh, angus, dear, all this talk about reading each other's memoirs, i don't want to get lost in the crowd – [see] Farrar Straus & Giroux "My Husband and My Wives" charles rowan beye, (oct 2, 2012) quick before it goes out of print! why can't we all be in périgord? much the best, my dear. i am eighty-four married to a man with whom i have been twenty five years dividing our time between massachusetts new york city and sarasota florida, now about to sell the house in massachusetts and concentrate on our studio on fifty seventh street and sarasota. these are the bland years. odd to be so old since parents died young and i had no model for this. am one of six siblings and each seems to enjoy perfect health until the ninetieth birthday then falls over and dies. used to love san francisco but last i was there was appalled at stepping over the bums, homeless, druggies what-ever trying to take a stroll in golden gate park, and then i knew that in reality i am mrs cleaver and all that she represents. i will never forget that kiss. could call it "the transgressive moment.:" naomi miller who witnessed it, has never been the same! love and kisses, charlie

On Apr 4, 2014, at 2:32 PM, Angus Whyte <anguswhyte@mac.com> wrote:

Dear Charlie,

What a pleasure to hear from you, and I'm glad you're still above the ground and doing well.

As for kisses, you may know that the original Aengus was the Gaelic God of Love. It's been an occasional burden to carry such a heritage, however I've done my best to shoulder it. The story goes that Aengus wandered the hills of Scotland distrib-uting kisses to his favorites, which then turned into doves which fluttered about the heads of the chosen few.

I am delighted that you remember our kiss as a "transgressive moment".

I met my current husband in Washington, DC in 1980. We had a little fling back then, and when I moved to L.A., he remained on the East Coast. We each had a couple of boyfriends after that, and in 1999 he moved to S.F., and we've been together ever since.

Our Spring is off to a good beginning, because this week we sold our properties in Hawaii, which we've had for eleven years. It became too much work and hassle to maintain things that far away. Meanwhile, I'll be celebrating my 77th birthday this coming Tuesday, and remaining healthy and engaged.

I'm now working on my next book, which will be all gay stories. I was thinking of calling it "My Seriously Gay Stories", but now I'm considering "Transgressive Moments." If you have an editor or agent to recommend, that would be truly helpful. I just ordered your book on Amazon, and it will be here next week. I can hardly wait!

And here we are, thom and I, at the De Young Museum on Valentine's Day of this year. [photo enclosed]

Upwards and onwards! XXA.

Begin forwarded message:
From: Charles Beye <chuckbeye@comcast.net>
Subject: Re: your memoir
Date: April 4, 2014 12:05:30 PM PDT
To: Angus Whyte <anguswhyte@mac.com>

oh, angus how gorgeous you look, extraordinary that the facial lineaments also revealing such personality have completely withstood the ravages of time. and the young gentleman at your side. good lord! i want to say one last thing about that kiss and why it was so dramatic a moment in my life. as you will read in my memoir if you do not already know in nauseating detail my history, gay sexual encounters began with puberty not then interrupted but diverted into a separate channel when i married. in that era as you may remember one could manage any number of separate, real and counterfeit personalities and identities. one of mine was of course a young charming father of four children married to an attractive architect wife and part of a group of other young married couples, and this was a perfectly valid, deeply felt, instinctive formation of my affections and erotics, which of course had nothing to do with the other charlie beye, although indeed many knew, suspected, or whatever, these strands twisted together in my body and psyche. when you took me in your arms and kissed me that evening i surrendered to the utter normalcy of your gesture and my response--here were two healthy, happy, handsome sexually active, engaged males exercising their god given right to respond to one another. but truth to tell i had never done such a thing in a nominally "heterosexual" setting, and for that reason as i responded to your mouth normally happily and completely i also knew that i was profoundly transgressing. naomi, our hostess, as you probably never knew was deeply upset. i myself was shaken, not that i think anyone realized. it was such a nothing moment for you. but not for me. i will never forget it. yes, i am very much above ground, currently with a terrible cold, dripping at the nose, all from going to manhattan a week or so ago, from our condo here in sarasota where i live with richard. we are old and decrepit as you will see from a photo at the altar when we got married which is in the memoir. our lives are all about going to the gym, then in the evening to a lot of theater, opera, symphony and musical what not, in an audience where ninety is probably the median age; thank god i can still walk about, and go on the airplane to manhattan where we have a studio and to london and madrid without richard who is not all that keen to be a culture vulture and as an introvert grows weary of all that talking. it is not a particularly interesting period of my life, but i certainly had good times for many, many years, so i do sit and read and count my blessings. love and kisses, charlie

On Apr 4, 2014, at 12:01 PM, Angus Whyte
<anguswhyte@mac.com> wrote:

Dear Charlie,

Merci pour l'explication de texte!

You know, Eddie [my boyfriend from 1962 to 1977] and I met in 1962 and fell instantly into bed. Then I went to Amsterdam for 63-64, and when I returned to SF, Eddie and I took up where we left off, which was still in bed.

It never occurred to me while we were living first in Cambridge for three years and subsequently in Boston for the next seven, that anyone didn't know we were a gay couple. It seemed so obvious to us! I certainly remember Naomi, and I never had a clue that she was deeply upset. And why, I wonder, was that? Probably because she was frustrated and without love and sex. Nor did I know that you were deeply shaken.

In any case, all these many years later, I'm delighted that you found Richard and have been together for twenty-five years.

My husband thom's parents live in St. Augustine, and we occasionally go there, because thom is his mother's favorite of her three children. I am not the daughter-in-law she and her husband expected, but after 33 years, she's more or less accustomed to it. We also have other friends in Florida: MTT and Joshua in Miami Beach (sometimes); Caren Copening in Palm Beach, Joe Hobbs in Naples, and several friends in Key West, who also have a house on Vieques, which we've never seen. Maybe later this year we'll plan a trip to that part of the world, because we've never visited Sarasota either.

Meanwhile, San Francisco has changed enormously since you were here. There are too many young people making outrageous sums of money and driving up rents and real estate costs. The City has been cleaned up considerably, the Embarcadero freeway was torn down years ago, and the waterfront areas have been upgraded and gentrified. The Presidio is no longer a military base, but a public/private entity, and its waterfront has been reclaimed as marshland, with trails, biking paths, and beaches. Further, there is a magisterial building boom going on, and all sorts of new residential facilities are opening up, which is helping clean up the mid-Market Street areas. Maybe you should consider a trip here one of these days.

Meanwhile, this has been a lovely day of pen-palling.

L and K back atcha,

XXAngus

No Wedding for Me

2015

Decades ago, when it became clear I was more gay than not, I had a peculiar realization not long afterward that I would never have a wedding. I would never have a bride in a white dress, never have a rowdy, disgusting bachelor party with all my best friends from high school and college, never make my mother Truly Happy; my sister would never have any nephews or nieces (and neither would I, in fact, because my sister is a dyke and was addressing most of the same issues as I was, at about the same time). I would never have to worry about whether the ceremony should be in a church or a temple, never have to decide whether to simply elope and keep the money, never have to worry about the colors of the bridesmaids' dresses. I wouldn't have the biggest worry of all, which is if she would really want me AFTER the first night. Given all that, I pretty much just put it out of my mind.

Every once in a while, when I was invited to a friend's wedding, and when I had bought wedding gifts for almost everyone I had ever known, many of them for the second or the third time, I had a little pang of regret that *they* will never be buying a wedding gift for me. And then later on, when they had children, I bought silver spoons or baby clothes for them because it was obvious that I would never be buying them for my *own* children.

And then, if you're like me, you remember all those weddings you attended. The first ones, when you were small, and how bizarre they were, with everyone dressed up and stressed out, and how they made you wear a coat and tie, which made you feel very adult and capable of sampling everyone's alcoholic drinks when they weren't paying attention.

When I was in grammar school, for extra income, my mother used to rent out our spare room to "college girls." I found it embarrassing but was unable to change the situation. These girls were attending Sacramento Junior College to learn cosmetology or to find a boyfriend, or, if they were extremely lucky, both. Many of them came from farms in the Central Valley, and they were called Vargas, or Diaz, or Ramos. A particularly lively girl, despite her triste-sounding name, Dolores Ramos, was one of my mother's favorites, and after she graduated from the college and returned to the farmlands, she and my mother stayed in touch.

When Dolores decided to marry, they held a major celebratory event, and, in addition to a large Catholic church wedding, an enormous Portuguese banquet took place in the local grange hall. An ethnic band played non-stop. The tables of food were endless; they offered multiple bars, dancing and major consumption of alcohol long into the night. I drank too many leftover cocktails and found myself tipsy for the first time, which was extremely enjoyable.

There followed Jewish weddings, Protestant weddings, even a couple of Baptist weddings, which were less amusing than the Portuguese weddings, even to my child's point of view, at the time. Subsequently I attended formal weddings, indoor weddings, hippie weddings in the California Redwood Groves, casual weddings, even a couple of last-minute, Nevada, shotgun weddings. The thing about all these weddings was that there was always a bride and a groom, no matter what the composition of the families involved, and every time I got through a service and a party, I thought, *Damn, it's too bad I'll never have one of these.*

Many years after my father died, my widowed mother met a man whom she decided to marry. At the time I was overseas working at a U.S. State Department job in Africa, and my mother chose to wait until my return to get married. When I returned, clothed in the aura of exotic adventure and well-heeled from my well-paid job, plus per-diem surpluses for "hardship service," I asked my mother what she would like best as a wedding gift. To my surprise, she announced she wanted to be remarried in Las Vegas, so I reserved air tickets for my mother, her groom, my dyke sister, and myself. We stayed in a fine hotel, my mother and her groom were married in a schlocky little chapel, and we all went out to dinner following the ceremony.

After dinner, there was some discussion as to what we might or ought to do. Eventually, my mother and her husband decided to return to the hotel. My sister and I went out, found a nightclub featuring performances by Louis Armstrong and Marlene Dietrich, and, for the first time in some twenty years, my sister wore a dress. At the table next to ours, an extremely handsome young man, probably in his mid-twenties, was seated with a diamond-encrusted woman, probably in her mid-seventies. During the Louis Armstrong performance, I had difficulty keeping my eyes off the young man, and at one point my sister, regarding the fellow I was looking at, gave me a poke in the ribs with her elbow and whispered, I thought too loudly, "Honey, when I get rich, I'll buy you one of *those*." Later, Marlene came onstage, first amid a group of chorus girls, each dressed in fishnet stockings, tuxedo jacket and top hat. My sister was mesmerized. During her second act, Marlene reappeared in her famous chain-link dress, which everyone in the world knew had cost $100,000. At that point, mesmerized, my sister went slack-jawed, and it was my turn because revenge, in truth, is sweet! I jabbed her in the ribs, even harder than she'd jabbed me, and said: "Honey, when I get rich, I'll buy *you* one of *those*."

Many years later, when a friend of my aunt's, a woman in her late sixties, decided on a large church wedding in Beverly Hills upon the occasion of her decision to marry her long-time paramour, following the death of her husband, not only was there a remarkably pretentious engraved invitation; important music was played, a horse and carriage processed the bride to the church, virginally clad in white, in happy remembrance of the first time she had married, while her hapless swain obviously had no say whatsoever in the high drama of these proceedings. When I told my then-boyfriend Mike about the invitation from my aunt to escort her to this wedding, I asked: "What on earth shall I wear to this circus?"

His answer was quick and brief: "Your dark blue Ralph Lauren suit and *all* your jewelry!"

I remember a particularly memorable nuptial occasion, which took place while I was at graduate school in Seattle. An extremely attractive and popular fellow called Jeff surprised most of his friends, and all of the gay ones, with the news that he intended to marry a woman. He followed up this veiled threat with a wedding invitation to all his past and present boyfriends and lovers, and there was a fillip to the actual ceremony when it was noticed that the best man was his lover of the moment. There occurred another instant when it seemed that all the men in the room realized, simultaneously, that every man there had been to bed with the groom as well as the best man. Clearly, Jeff had planned for that to happen, but it was, in my experience, an All-Time-First, and I was impressed by his *savoir-faire.*

In Normandy, some years later, I attended a three-day wedding celebration carefully planned by my friend Pamela's parents in Boston. Complicated arrangements, including trans-atlantic flights and hotel reservations, were made months in advance. During the event, there was a series of endless lunches and dinners, enormous quantities of cider, wine, and Calvados, plus another horse-and-carriage procession, this one enhanced with the presence of a phalanx of liveried musicians playing hunting horns at the entrance to the country chapel in which the ceremony was to be held. Pamela's wedding was followed by an *al-fresco* luncheon for the entire village, on the grounds of the church.

In Bali I was invited to a wedding where the bride, groom and their families and guests all wore sarongs, because not to do so would have been a mark of disrespect. That, I found, was a dramatic difference in wedding attire.

It was many years later I attended my first gay wedding. Both grooms, Alan and Jeffrey, were Jewish, the ceremony took place outdoors in an elegant country setting under a traditional huppah. Members of both families were present, as was a rabbi for each of the grooms, and the wedding was traditional. The event was catered, pink cloths graced the tables, and everyone enjoyed full bars, music, and dancing. It was not so different from a bar mitzvah, but a lot more fun. The fellow I was living with at the time sat with someone else during the ceremony, got drunk at the party, and embarrassed me beyond description.

All in all, weddings were not my favorite things, and not only because I thought I would never have one. In 1999, however, everything changed. I had the good fortune to get involved with a fellow whom I had known for almost twenty years. When I first met thom, he was twenty-one and I was forty-three. There was an instant spark, and we remained friends ever since. In the meantime, thom and I lived on opposite coasts and we both went through several long-term relationships. In 1999, we found ourselves single and, to cut the story short, decided to become an item. We have been living together since, quite happily and comfortably, because we both really like each other and, I believe most importantly, because there is no issue about trust. We have been friends for so long we have no secrets and no problem communicating. We trust each other completely, we have nothing to hide and can't pretend we are any different from what we are, so there's no pretense, no dissimulation, and no foolish gamesmanship.

In 2000, we were invited to Vermont on July first for a memorial celebration. As we drove from Manhattan north to New Hampshire on June 30th, we listened on the radio to NPR's story on Vermont's new law legitimizing civil unions for committed gay and lesbian couples, scheduled to take place for the first time anywhere in the United States on July first—the next day. We discussed the issue and decided it would be a good thing for us to do. Then, when we arrived at our hosts' place in Hanover, NH, a big party was going on, so we had no opportunity to talk about the subject or get further information. The following morning our hosts, Jon and Darrell, announced: "We're taking you to our favorite pond for a swim, in Norwich, across the river in Vermont." So off we went, picnic and dog in tow.

In the middle of the pond, I asked Darrell, "So, if one wanted to have a civil union here, what would be necessary?"

He replied: "I think you just go to a town clerk's office and fill out the forms."

I then asked: "Is there a town clerk in Norwich?"

He pulled out his cell phone, dialed a number, and said: "Roxanne, are you there?" She replied in the affirmative, and he told her he had two friends who were interested in a CU. She informed him that the office was open until noon, and he asked: "What time is it now?"

"Eleven thirty-six," she answered.

So we jumped out of the pond, climbed into our cutoffs and t-shirts, drove into Norwich, found the town clerk's office, filled out the forms, and, with the gracious assistance of Roxanne and her colleague in the office, procured the services of a justice of the peace for that very afternoon. We then bought champagne, returned to the pond, finished our picnic and engaged our friends to join us and witness our ceremony.

The justice of the peace, Ernie, lived in a secluded country house, with a manicured yard and a stunning view over Mt. Killington. Ernie was nervous because he had never previously performed a ceremony for two guys. Fortunately, Roxanne and her colleague had given us a sample text, so we had something to begin with, which Ernie found reassuring. One of our friends, Todd, went around the yard and picked two bouquets of wildflowers, one for thom and one for me. Jon, who is a professional photographer, grabbed my camera and took photographs all during the ceremony. Darrell, meanwhile, kept us all in line. Because this had happened so suddenly, neither of us had been able to find rings, so we decided to use the rings we already had and deal with proper wedding rings later.

The ceremony took place on the lawn, and, if you had ever asked me beforehand what my wedding would be like, I would have told you it would be extremely well-organized, very proper, with everyone dressed up, special music, and excellent food and wine. What happened was an impromptu ceremony on the lawn with only three friends present, no music at all, and everyone except Ernie in cutoffs and t-shirts. The sun was shining, birds were singing, and everyone was in a festive mood. Our ceremony was simple and remarkably moving. Thom and I clutched our bouquets of wildflowers, and when the words were concluded, everybody kissed everybody else, except for Ernie, who was still unaccustomed to the idea. We did not promise to "honor" or "obey," but what brought mist to my eyes was hearing myself say, "I, Angus, take you, thom, to be my spouse in our civil union, to have and to hold from this day on, for better, for worse, for richer, for poorer, to love and to cherish forever," and to hear thom say the same things to me. Odd as it once may have seemed, I knew in the depths of my heart it was true.

San Francisco, September, 2000

P.S. thom likes to describe himself as a "serial nuptualist," and, since the year 2000, the world has changed significantly. It is now legal for gay and lesbian couples to marry in Holland, Belgium, Spain, New Zealand, and Canada. In 2003 we were married in Toronto, a civil service recognized as legal except in the United States. Last week, we were married once again, in our home city of San Francisco, given that the State of California has allowed legal gay and lesbian weddings since June of this year.

San Francisco, September, 2008

P.P.S. Things have changed rapidly since 2008, and now, according to the *New York Times*:

• June 26, 2015 WASHINGTON — In a long-sought victory for the gay rights movement, the Supreme Court ruled by a 5-to-4 vote on Friday that the Constitution guarantees a right to same-sex marriage.

"No longer may this liberty be denied," Justice Anthony M. Kennedy wrote for the majority in the historic decision. "No union is more profound than marriage, for it embodies the highest ideals of love, fidelity, devotion, sacrifice and family. In forming a marital union, two people become something greater than once they were."

Marriage is a "keystone of our social order," Justice Kennedy said, adding that the plaintiffs in the case were seeking "equal dignity in the eyes of the law."

The decision, which was the culmination of decades of litigation and activism, set off jubilation and tearful embraces across the country, the first same-sex marriages in several states, and resistance at least stalling in others. It came against the backdrop of fast-moving changes in public opinion, with polls indicating that most Americans now approve of the unions.

The Accident

2016

Thom and I met in Washington, D.C., in 1980, when I moved there to open an art gallery. It was our mutual friend, Addison Lee, who invited him to dinner at my house on Capitol Hill. He likes to tell people he ended up as dessert. He was, in fact, delicious. We became good friends during my year in D.C., which I found unsatisfactory as a business venture, and at the end of the year I sublet the gallery and moved to Los Angeles. Thom remained in and around Washington, and for several years thereafter we would meet at least once a year, if not in D.C., in Boston, New York, Mexico, France, San Francisco, or Los Angeles.

It was late December of 1998 when we agreed to meet in New York and drive to Walnut Hill Retreat in Raymond, New Hampshire, for a program entitled "New Year Visions" sponsored by the Body Electric School. Thom had just purchased a new Toyota and offered to drive us up to New Hampshire, along with another friend, Lee, who was attending the same retreat.

The retreat facility was seriously impoverished, and the guest rooms were almost barren. Upon arrival, we discussed leaving at once, then decided to soldier on, given the effort expended to get there. A lunch was served, followed by the usual greetings, a heart circle, discussions about what each of us wanted to gain from the experience, and what we were hoping for the new year following.

We were scheduled to depart the Sunday following our arrival, and I was already committed to a dinner party that same evening at one of the best restaurants in Manhattan, Jean-Georges. I was looking forward to meeting the chef and enjoying an extraordinary meal with an old friend who knew the chef and planned the dinner.

As usual, I took notes, beginning on the first day of the program, and from the moment we arrived, I was miserable. It was freezing cold outside, hot and dry inside. We slept badly on a rotten mattress on the floor, awakened during the night over and over, due to creaking boards on the stairways, then awakened early in dismay. The place was tacky and ugly, and it was difficult to believe it was "Sacred Space," as advertised. I had a terrible crick in my back and only sleeping with thom made it bearable. I have an expectation that gay surroundings will be esthetically pleasing, and when they're not, I'm uncomfortable.

In addition to the mattress on the floor issue, the water pressure was weak, the bathing facilities inadequate, and my inner bitch was highly critical. Especially since the meals were sparse and unsatisfactory. My only solace was a thought that if it's so bad at the beginning, with luck it will improve. Sometimes a point of view can be changed.

It was halfway through the first day before I began to feel all right, as the facilitator asked us to begin with what each of us was aware of with Heart, Body, Soul, and Spirit on the final day of the year.

My heart was still in pain from the loss of my previous boyfriend, Andreas, and I was glad for thom, Terry, Bruce, Mark, Mike and my other good men who composed my Logical Family, as opposed to my Biological Family, and I longed for a partner, lover, sweetheart, and soulmate, and when I put voice to that thought, someone in the group responded: "These people should never meet."

It was Winter, and I felt my body needed some attention, with more aerobic exercise, biking, running, and swimming. I felt my soul was on a changing path, to be more open, more questing, and more vulnerable.

My spirit was generally good, except for occasional bouts of anger, melancholy, fear, or despair—none of which was long-lasting or debilitating. My critical faculties were frequently working overtime, and there was more attention necessary with Acceptance and Forgiveness.

The most satisfying result of the day's exercises was the feeling I have untold reservoirs of love—and there is hope for getting what I want.

During last night's exercises, I realized what I most wanted to be rid of was my inability to forgive the man who had left me fifteen months earlier. It was a long process, still incomplete. Spending New Year's Eve doing rituals with twenty-four naked men is both a mental and physical concentration, as well as a soul and spirit concentration. The group dancing following the rituals was joyous, tender, spirited, affectionate, playful, and liberating.

The morning's work was two-on-one massage, back only, using cornstarch instead of oil or lotion. The question to ponder between back massage and anal massage is: what is my body telling me? Mine is telling me I'm in good health and shape for my age. It's also telling me to lose five or ten pounds and do more exercise. It's telling me to enjoy it more and use it more. All of it!

The afternoon session was devoted to anal massage, something quite different from penetration or fucking. It is sensual, sensitive, gentle, hygienic, relaxing, and pleasurable. The facilitator exclaimed: "We can't be whole until we reclaim our holes."

Dinner was a dress up event: costumes, drag, fantasy, or all the above. Very silly and quite funny. The evening session was prefaced with an essay about dance as a healing art. We did expressive dancing alone, then together as a group, followed by drumming, more dancing, and singing for a long time. Everyone seemed really into it, but I thought it went on too long. Further, I couldn't imagine how people can do this without drugs. By then I was exhausted, because last night we all stayed up until three o'clock.

Question for the New Year: How can I love and nourish myself in 1999?

The morning ritual was devoted to self-pleasuring, first with blindfolds, self-massage, and music, leading to a Big Draw. As usual, I feel sex is incomplete without ejaculation, even though I know that is precisely the point of tantric sex. This new year of exploration is not easy or comfortable for many of us, yet we're approaching it from a compassionate and loving way within this "instant community." Would that the rest of the world might experience this expansion of soul and spirit in such a generous and nurturing environment!

The sun was beaming into a room of shiny, oil-covered, naked men in silent contemplation. Thom is beneath the window, limned by sunlight, looking like a sculpture by Canova. Outside it's five degrees and Nicholas is stretched out on his red and blue striped towel, as though he were on a beach in Australia.

Prayers for the planet in the New Year: that all war budgets be redirected to education and the welfare of human beings rather than to fear and destruction.

Hopes, Dreams and Intentions for my Communities: neighborhood improvement and beautification, funding goal for our LGBT capital campaign, establishment of my philanthropic project, Art for Healing, on a solid financial basis, generosity towards others who are in need in my personal community.

Personal desires and wishes: love and intimacy in my personal life with a person who shares my values, closure with Andreas, some kind of reconnection with my sister on mutually acceptable terms, search for a larger living space in San Francisco, search for a larger gallery and storage space for Art for Healing, long-range financial planning, serenity and good health for family, anger control about my sister, consciousness-raising for Andreas, less pain for my ailing Aunt El, a personal life for Mark, a reciprocated love for Stephen, a breakdown of barriers for Bruce, good health for Mike, satisfaction for Robert, romance for Karen, freedom from money concerns for us all so we may concentrate on other matters.

Heart's Desire: to share my life and passions with a soulmate, to live free of anxiety, fear, and anger, to enjoy the Eternal Now, to have the best of whatever I have, to remain healthy, to regain my vision, to be grateful for what I have, to maintain a sense of humor and equilibrium, no matter what.

At four o'clock, as darkness began to settle in, fifteen of us set off for the sweat lodge, wearing as many layers of clothing as possible. John, the facilitator, had been there most of the afternoon keeping a fire burning to heat the stones. We walked in silence, arriving at a blazing bonfire in the snow. Offerings were made to the fire, after which we stripped and were ceremonially smudged with burning sage. A preliminary bucket of red-hot stones was placed into the fire pit inside the lodge, and we entered in single file to sit on wooden benches in a circle around the fire pit. The sweat lodge was built of timbers at the base, with a roof of slightly translucent fabric stretched over a frame of branches. Water was poured on the hot stones to create steam, and the ceremonies began. First, an invocation to the earth, sky, winds, sun, and moon, and the four directions, punctuated with chanting and deep breathing. Additional invocations were made to various spirits, along with prayers and supplications, first by the leader, and subsequently by each participant, in succession. Each utterance was followed by a deep breath and a ceremonial sound, like "ohhmm," in different registers. Because of the restricted space, the sounds reverberated intensely.

Prayers and supplications were offered to the earth, our communities, our families and friends, to our loved ones, present and departed, and to each of us present. Each series was followed by a song or chant which we had previously learned, and each song or chant was preceded by an additional bucketful of hot stones. As the temperature rose, so did the intensity of the songs and chants. Some of the prayers were general, others quite specific. Some very moving, others banal. All were accorded equal respect and acknowledgment.

The feeling of sitting naked in a sweat lodge in the snow-covered forest, doing rituals with spirit brothers is powerful. Atavistic emotions and feelings are easily and readily provoked, in accompaniment to the outpouring of sweat and prayer, leading to an intimacy of camaraderie and spirit better experienced than described. The ritual lasted about two hours, and at the close, everyone emerged into the cold, rubbed down with an icy towel, and dressed silently and as quickly as possible before the fire. The equipment was assembled, and we all filed back to the retreat building in silence, strangely moved.

———ℰℛℬ———

We awakened the next morning to snow falling, dropping temperatures, and the prospect of a final lunch planned for noon just before departure. Having lived in New England for many years, I said to thom and to Lee, "We have to leave right now, before the roads get too icy." They both complained and insisted we stay for lunch before departure to complete the retreat agenda. I was in the minority and outvoted, despite my misgivings. Because of the weather conditions, at departure I drove very slowly and carefully, heading from Raymond on Route 102 towards I-93 and south to New York City.

Fifteen or twenty minutes down the road, on a stretch of highway with a guard rail on the right, we were struck head on by a large vehicle skidding on a patch of black ice. It careened off the highway, then careened back on, crossing the median. Because of the guard rail, we had no way we could escape or pull off the highway. Our seat belts functioned well and so did the airbags. Thom and I, luckily, had buckled up and were mostly unhurt. Lee, in the back seat, had not buckled up, struck his head and was unconscious.

While thom attended to Lee, I saw no movement in the other vehicle and got out to open its passenger door. A blond youth was slumped over the steering wheel with blood running down his face and his eyes closed. I was wondering if he was alive, and, slowly, he opened his eyes and whispered, "Are you all right?" Instantly, I fell in love with him.

Meanwhile, passers-by had stopped and called police and ambulances, which arrived within fifteen minutes. They gave oxygen to Lee, put him on a stretcher, strapped him on a gurney, and put him in the first ambulance. I had chest pains and a bruised hand, but I was mobile. The second ambulance took Daniel, the driver of the vehicle which hit ours, and the third one took me, and because of possible neck or spine injuries, I was put into a cervical collar and strapped down, while thom rode along.

We were all taken to the hospital in Derry and given X-rays and EKGs. Lee was given a CAT scan in case of possible brain damage. Our clothing was completely soaked from standing in the cold rain, so they gave us hospital robes and blankets to wear. The Fire Department was assisted by local volunteer helpers who seemed like angels. The medical teams were quick and efficient, and nurses and doctors arrived swiftly.

We all helped each other, and there wasn't a single word of blame or recrimination. Immediately after the accident, I said to thom, "I'm so sorry about your new car." (It was only three months old.)

He replied, "It's only a car. I'm so glad we're all alive."

Daniel was devastated and kept saying, "It's my fault, it's my fault."

And I kept telling him, "It's not your fault, it was an *accident* caused by ice on the road." Thom kept talking to Lee until he was able to respond, although he didn't know who or where he was for some time.

Eventually thom telephoned his parents, Lee telephoned his mother and his brother, Daniel called his mother and his girl-friend, and I realized there was no one to call, which seemed odd. At the same time, I realized I was not seriously injured, and it probably didn't matter, but it was something to notice.

Both vehicles were totaled and towed to a lot. Daniel's mother, Margaret, arrived at the hospital about three fifteen and remained there for hours, until we were all treated and discharged. Margaret insisted we all return to her house, and since we had no clothes or car and it was getting dark, we agreed. We piled into her car and stopped first at a market. She asked what we wanted for dinner, and I requested, "Steaks, please, and a large quantity of red wine." She kindly obliged, drove us home, gave me and thom a guest room, washed our clothes because we had nothing to wear, and put Lee on a sofa, where I was charged to check on him every four hours through the night in case there were problems with his concussion.

While Lee, Daniel, and I were being treated, thom dealt with the police, the tow truck people, and the insurance company. Daniel had neither medical nor auto insurance, and although his leg was cut open to the bone, it was a miracle he wasn't hurt more seriously, given that he hadn't been wearing a seat belt. After dinner, Lee, Margaret, her husband Richard, and Daniel watched TV while I took a long bath and lay down quietly.

I set the alarm for four hours later, went to check on Lee, and he was half-awake, conscious, groggy, and sporting a healthy erection. We talked a bit, I determined he was going to be fine by morning and decided to cheer him up with a nocturnal blowjob since there was really nothing else to do. He was grateful for my non-traditional, medical intervention.

Thom was amused when I told him what had transpired, and after breakfast the next morning, we reserved a car at the Manchester airport. Margaret drove us, first to the wrecking lot in Derry, then back to the body shop where our car was towed. The trunk was forced open so we could retrieve our luggage and belongings.

We transferred the luggage into the rental car and drove to NYC, arriving at six o'clock that evening. Lee went to his mother's, thom and I went to our friend Carol's, where we were invited to stay, and two hours later Carol took me to the best restaurant in the City, Jean-Georges, where she had made reservations weeks ahead of time.

Since then, I haven't returned to New Hampshire, although I did keep in touch with Margaret, and two Christmases later she told me sorrowfully that Daniel had taken his own life. What a terrible waste, I felt. He was only twenty-four years old.

Following our short sojourn in New York, thom went back to Arlington, VA, where he lived, and I returned home to San Francisco. Then, later that year, he telephoned to say he had decided to move to California. And a month or two later he drove across the country and arrived in San Francisco during one of the great real estate booms, when it was almost impossible to find an apartment, and people queued thirty or forty deep whenever a vacancy was announced. One of our good friends had just moved into a large house and welcomed him there for the first two months. Then I asked him to come with me to a gathering of friends in Palm Springs, and we drove down in my recently acquired classic Mercedes, talking on the way about our lives, how our friendship had lasted for so many years, and what we hoped for in the future. I asked him what he was looking for in a partner, and, not surprisingly, it was pretty much what I wanted, as well.

Then he asked, "Is this a proposition?"

I retorted, "I wasn't exactly thinking that, but it might be, depending . . ."

"Depending on what?" he asked.

I said: "If the answer is yes, it's a proposition. If it's no, I don't know what you're talking about."

We both laughed, and he admitted a fear that a relationship might harm our friendship. After a bit more "gay repartee," we decided to try it out for a month or two. It's now seventeen years later, and in 2000 we went to Vermont for a Civil Union, when it was first proposed and allowed. Subsequently we were legally married in Canada in 2003, then again legally married in California in 2008. Thom describes us as "serial nuptualists." I still wonder if the accident had somehow dramatically and literally thrown us together, given the fragility of life we experienced with that close call there in New Hampshire.

And since then, we never drive without fastening our seat belts.

If you enjoyed *The Lavender Blade,* please consider leaving your review at amazon.com where you can find Angus Whyte's original book of short stories *After - Dinner Tales.*

About the Author

A native Californian, Angus Whyte (1937-2019) lived in San Francisco following his graduation from University of California at Berkeley in the late 1950s. He enrolled in graduate studies at the University of Washington, where he earned a Master's degree in French and Music. In 1959, he was awarded a Fulbright Teaching Scholarship in France, and, in the early 1960s, contracted with the U.S. State Department to teach public health via mobile cinema in the Congo Republic. He subsequently studied baroque music and harpsichord at the Amsterdam Conservancy and the Salzburg Mozarteum Academy.

In the 1970s he operated the Angus Whyte Fine Arts Gallery in Boston, Provincetown, MA, New York City, and Washington, DC. After completing the Institute of Arts Administration program at Harvard University, he worked as Director of Special Events at Art Center College of Design in Pasadena, CA in the 1980s, during which he served on the boards of the Brody Arts Foundation, Pacific Serenades, and the California Confederation of the Arts.

Following a sabbatical in France in the early 1990s, where he renovated ancient stone buildings in the Périgord, he returned to San Francisco, where he served as development consultant to the capital campaign for the LGBT Community Center Project. From 1997 through 2012 he directed a philanthropic organization, Art for Healing, which placed donated original works of art in hospitals and healthcare facilities.

In 2013 he published "After-Dinner Tales", his first collection of memoirs, recollections, essays, observations and vignettes drawn from his extraordinary life. Upon his move to Palm Springs, CA in 2017, he remained active in music and arts circles, and joined the Palm Springs Writers Guild as he crafted the stories found in this collection.

More of Angus' stories can be found at www.anguswhyte.com.

CPSIA information can be obtained
at www.ICGtesting.com
Printed in the USA
BVHW071705150421
605031BV00007B/551

9 781954 604018